9AP

Sam Skelly
510 547 2851

FLUSH
DECKS
&
FOUR
PIPES

JOHN D. ALDEN

Commander
U.S. Navy
(Retired)

NAVAL INSTITUTE PRESS
Annapolis, Maryland

Revised printing, 1989

Library of Congress Catalogue Card No. 65-15296

ISBN 0-87021-186-2

Printed in the United States of America

Designed by Walter Paiko

Unless otherwise indicated,
all photographs are Official U.S. Navy

It may be trite to characterize this book as a labor of love, but it would be incorrect to describe it otherwise. I never served on any destroyer, let alone a flush decker, and the James Alden for whom DD-211 was named is not a known relative of mine. However, I was born into a household where these destroyers were a part of daily life. My father was on the staff of Commander, Destroyer Squadrons, U.S. Pacific Fleet at San Diego, and my arrival was recognized by the presentation of a silver cup and bowl from his messmates on the staff and the flagship *Charleston* (Cruiser No. 22). A few years later we were in Hawaii, where my father had become navigator of the fast minelayer *Ludlow* (DM-10). As a result, family tales of my early years frequently involved such ships as the *Wickes* (DD-75) and *Woolsey* (DD-77), the old *Brooklyn* (Armored Cruiser No. 3), the *Chaumont* (AP-5), and the *Burns* (DM-11).

My first recollection of an actual flush decker was as a Navy brat being invited on board one for supper at Mare Island Navy Yard. I still remember the hum of the blowers and the smells of machinery and of chow cooking in the galley.

Flash forward to World War II. There was usually a flush decker around New London when I was undergoing submarine training, and my ship, the *Lamprey* (SS-372), encountered others as tame targets for dummy torpedoes or as escorts into port. Later, while serving on the *Sea Cat* (SS-399), I was surprised to find a former flush decker, the *Teapa* (ex-*Putnam* DD-287), unloading bananas in Miami.

It was not until still later, when I was stationed at the Bureau of Ships in Washington, that my fascination with ships led me to start writing for the *U.S. Naval Institute Proceedings*. Ready access to the Navy's historical records, which were then only a few wings away in the old Main Navy building, gave me ideal opportunities for casual research, and I began to track down the unusual histories of some of the flush deckers. There were so many of them that I conceived the idea of writing an article covering the whole class.

Unfortunately, my first draft produced puzzlement at the Naval Institute; it was too long for an article but too short for a book. Could I perhaps expand it? Not much chance; I was on active duty and had little free time for outside writing. Then the Institute decided to start a new series of publications known as Sea Power Monographs, and I was encouraged to rework my material on the flush deckers as one of these. So, under the stern guidance and critical review of editor Frank Uhlig, Jr., this book emerged some four years later.

Since *Flush Decks and Four Pipes* was first published, I have enjoyed hearing from scores of former destroyer sailors. Many recalled incidents from their own experiences, always with expressions of great affection for their old ships. Several were able to fill in gaps in the record or point out new sources of information. Their contributions appear in the addenda to this edition. A few readers took exception to the unusual binding adopted by the publisher, and I must admit that I too have found it unhandy at times. I am doubly pleased, therefore, that the Naval Institute Press has decided to reprint my book and to do it in a more conventional format. I hope it will continue to recall fond memories among those who sailed in the old flush-deck four-pipers and, perhaps, show younger generations a bit about the professional dedication, ingenuity, and hardiness of those who served the Navy in times past.

If there has ever been such a thing in the history of the United States Navy as a typically American class of ship, the flush-deck destroyers of World War I come closest to filling the bill. They made their appearance in every part of the world between the years 1917 and 1947, their distinctive silhouette unmistakably proclaiming them "made in America." These ships performed in an extraordinary variety of roles during their long and useful collective life. Built too late for much combat service in World War I, they had become obsolescent by the outbreak of World War II, but were still indispensable. Between wars, the weight of their numbers served as a damper on all new United States destroyer construction for twelve years, and in their later years their very existence as usable hulls all but forced the Navy to find unconventional uses for them. This chronicle is intended to be an outline history of these ships as a class and a record of the metamorphoses undergone by them in the course of reassignment and conversion, rather than a collection of operational histories of the individual ships, however glorious these may have been.

Some readers may wonder why the class was not referred to in the preceding paragraph as "four pipers," as the ships commonly were called during their lifetime. It will be seen that the term "flush decker" is descriptive of every ship in the class, while "four piper" is not. A number of earlier destroyers had four stacks also, but not all the flush deckers did. Three of the class were built with only three stacks and served out their careers in this abbreviated rig, while many others in later life were deprived of one or two of their original stacks. But there is no record of any of these ships ever having had other than a flush weather deck. Hence the terminology.

The flush-deck feature, a radical departure from the high forecastle, broken-deck arrangement of the "thousand tonners" and other early destroyers, was introduced to obtain added strength amidships while still keeping the customary draft and freeboard forward and aft. Experience had demonstrated the necessity for high freeboard forward for seakeeping, and low freeboard aft in order to keep the silhouette as low as possible. The latter feature also eased the handling of depth charges, though such weapons were not anticipated when our World War I destroyers were designed.

It is customary to think of the flush deckers as "peas in a pod" members of a mass production, war emergency construction program. To some extent they were, but there was an amazing number of variations in the group even as built. Of the 273 ships completed between the numbers of DD-69 and DD-347 inclusive (hull numbers 200-205 were canceled prior to construction), the first six were experimental in nature, and thus in certain respects never did resemble their later near-sisters. All six had cutaway sterns instead of the raked cruiser type common to the rest of the class. Of this group, *Caldwell* (DD-69), *Craven* (DD-70), and *Manley* (DD-74) had four stacks. The real "sports" were *Gwin*, *Conner*, and *Stockton* (DD-71 to 73), which had only three smoke pipes, with the center one thicker than its mates.

Conner and *Stockton* also had three propeller shafts. The shaft and turbine arrangement was quite unusual by modern standards, and the machinery was located in a single engine room. The two outboard shafts were connected to combined low pressure and astern, direct drive, Parsons turbines. The center shaft had the main turbine coupled directly to it, but forward of this turbine was a clutch and reduction gear into which a fourth turbine for cruising was coupled. This peculiar rig, not to mention the direct drive turbines, which were of old-fashioned design even at the time they were installed, must have been something of a puzzle to the U.S. and British crews who recommissioned the ships a generation later.

Additional differences among the 273 ships, though minor in outward appearance, came about because of the participation of eleven different building yards in the construction program. After the first six experimental ships, two basic plans were evolved. The numerous Bethlehem Steel yards all followed one plan, while the rest of the builders used another plan, developed by Bath Iron Works. But in all cases, the building yards made slight changes to accommodate their own particular practices. Mare Island Navy Yard built the lead ship, *Caldwell*, and 14 others. Other navy yards were sparsely represented, with four ships by Norfolk, and the lone *Tillman* (DD-135) by Charleston. The bulk of the class was civilian-built. *Gwin* (DD-71) was the sole entry from Seattle Construction and Dry Dock Company. Bath Iron Works built 12; Newport

A flush decker speeds through a beam sea as she lays smoke. Note wake of the ship ahead, masts of the ship astern. The tall mainmast, later removed, identifies this ship as one of the early flush deckers. The higher-numbered ships always had short mainmasts.

1

News Shipbuilding and Dry Dock Company, 25; New York Shipbuilding Corporation, at Camden, New Jersey, 30; and William Cramp & Sons at Philadelphia, 48. The various Bethlehem Steel yards carried off the largest share of the program, with 35 at the Squantum, Massachusetts, yard (specially erected for the purpose with covered sheds enclosing the shipways and fitting-out basins), 36 at the old Fore River yard at Quincy, and 66 at San Francisco (Union Iron Works). As a rule, each builder used different types of turbines and boilers, adding to the differences between the ships.

In designed standard displacement, they varied from 1,020 to 1,190 tons. Their "normal" displacement, the designed figure for a ship fully equipped and ready for sea, varied from 1,125 to 1,215 tons. Actual trial displacements of the ships as built ranged up to 1,370 tons. World War II alterations resulted in displacements of up to 1,700 tons.

All the hull dimensions were within a few inches of 314 by 31 feet, an extremely "fine" hull ratio even for destroyers, which as a type are long, narrow ships. Rated draft was 9 feet 10 inches. As previously noted, the ships of the first series, DD-69 through 74, were experimental; but the second group, DD-75 through 185, was standardized and built to meet a guaranteed speed. These ships generally met or exceeded their designed speed and were within their planned displacements. By the time the third group (DD-186 through 347) was contracted for, the war crisis was at hand and the best power plants could not always be obtained, nor were time and skilled workmen available to permit the refinements of construction called for in the earlier ships. The only performance guaranteed was the delivery of the specified shaft horsepower. In actuality, the 186 class averaged around five or six per cent overweight. The different power plants in the various classes produced a range of shaft horsepower between 19,700 and 27,000 for rated speeds of 32 to 35 knots. *Branch* (DD-197) was credited officially with the fastest heels of the class, with a trial speed of 36.48 knots, although *Hale* (DD-133) claimed to have beaten this by logging an average of 37.1 knots on a record run, in 1919, from Hamburg, Germany, to Harwich, England. The earlier ships, through DD-185, had a fuel capacity of 275 tons, nominally equivalent to a cruising range of 4,300 miles at 14 knots, and were referred to as being "short-legged." The later, "long-legged" ships,

with machinery in good shape and a clean bottom, could steam 5,000 miles on 375 tons of oil, also at 14 knots.

In armament, the usual suit was four 4-inch/50 single-purpose rifles, a lone 3-inch/23 antiaircraft gun, and several machine guns. The big punch consisted of twelve 21-inch torpedo tubes in triple mounts. The torpedo mounts were staggered; two on either beam. The position of the after four-incher varied. Originally mounted on the fantail, it was moved to the roof of the after deckhouse when the lower position was found too wet. The position of the antiaircraft gun also varied; on the early ships it was usually just forward of the bridge, and later, on the fantail. On some ships it was on the after deckhouse. In the early years, some ships carried two 3-inch/23s. There were also many minor variations in the number and location of the smaller armament, which consisted of up to three 1-pounders or .30 caliber machine guns or some combination thereof. By 1921 two or three .30 calibers was the standard light battery. The only major differences occurred in *Hovey* and *Long* (DD-208 and 209) which carried eight 4-inch/50s in twin mounts, and the 231-235 group—*Hatfield, Brooks, Gilmer, Fox,* and *Kane*—with four 5-inch/51s for a main battery. The 5-inch armament was adopted to meet the threat posed by German U-boat cruisers which were armed with 5.9-inch guns; but, of course, the 5-inch guns never had the opportunity for a combat test. Early in her career the three-stack, three-screw *Stockton* carried five 4-inch/50s in a twin mount forward and three singles elsewhere. By 1922, when she went out of commission for 18 years, her twin mount had been replaced by a single. *Semmes* (DD-189) also mounted for a time one twin and three single 4-inch guns.

Caldwell, although the lowest numbered, was beaten out for first commissioning by *Manley,* which was commissioned on 15 October 1917, and *Stockton,* which hoisted her pennant on 26 November. Thereafter, the others followed in rapid succession. Last to enter service was *Decatur* (DD-341) on 9 August 1922, almost two years behind *Pruitt* (DD-347), the highest numbered of them all.

Mare Island set something of an all-time record in construction in 1918. By careful assembly of material and maximum use of prefabrication, the yard put *Ward* (DD-139) together in 17 days from keel-laying to launching, with commissioning less

Flush-deck destroyers under construction at the New York Shipbuilding Corporation yard in Camden, New Jersey. Closest ship is Dickerson, next is Leary, succeeding four probably are Schenck, Herbert, Brooks, and Hatfield. Farthermost destroyer is De Long. Numbers on sterns are the builder's hull numbers, not Navy DD numbers. Note the curious shape on the third ship's after deckhouse.

than two months later. The only approach to this performance was by the Squantum yard, which launched *Reid* (DD-292) 36 days after keel-laying, and commissioned her 49 days after that. The construction of almost all the class was hurried, and the workmanship unfortunately was not always first class. Commander Joseph K. Taussig, who put *Little* (DD-79) in commission, recorded that leaky seams and loose rivets were the rule; boiler tubes had to be re-rolled wholesale; and a bushel basketful of nuts and bolts was collected from inside steam and water lines during shakedown. These items generally made their presence known by lodging under valve seats during critical evolutions, such as backing down for an emergency stop. Some such deficiencies were probably at the root of a casualty which cost two lives on *Flusser* (DD-289) when a steam line ruptured in June 1920.

The list of first commanding officers of these ships reads like a roster of the high command of World War II, with names such as McCandless, Fletcher, Giffen, Spruance, Powell, W. A. Lee, Norman Scott, Rosendahl, and Halsey standing out. Lieutenant Commander C. E. Rosendahl, later to win lighter-than-air fame, had the unique distinction of placing no fewer than four of the flush deckers in commission, one after another, within a period of less than six months. This was in 1920-21, when the new craft were going almost directly from the fitting-out pier to a lay-up berth.

The names of the 273 ships, besides commemorating most of the Navy's heroes and benefactors, included a number of "twins" with identical last names, and one set of triplets. To minimize the confusion resulting from similar nomenclature, many of these ships were christened with the given and middle names or initials of their namesakes. Thus there were:

Ward (DD-139) and *Aaron Ward* (DD-132)
Badger (DD-126) and *George E. Badger* (DD-196)
Upshur (DD-144) and *Abel P. Upshur* (DD-193)
Hamilton (DD-141) and *Paul Hamilton* (DD-307)
Edwards (DD-265) and *John D. Edwards* (DD-216)
Wood (DD-317) and *Welborn C. Wood* (DD-195)
Thompson (DD-305) and *Smith Thompson* (DD-212)
Preston (DD-327) and *William B. Preston* (DD-344)
and the three Joneses, *Jacob Jones* (DD-130), *Paul Jones* (DD-230), and *William Jones* (DD-308).

Several others, although not identical in spelling, were similar enough to warrant carrying distinguishing first names:

Burns (DD-171) and *John Francis Burnes* (DD-299)
Ingraham (DD-111) and *Osmond Ingram* (DD-255)
Talbot (DD-114) and *J. Fred Talbott* (DD-156)
Lea (DD-118) and *S. P. Lee* (DD-310)

Robert Smith (DD-324) and *James K. Paulding* (DD-238) were so named to distinguished them from *Smith* (DD-17) and *Paulding* (DD-22) of older classes still in service. *Rizal* (DD-174), named for the Philippine patriot, was the only one so to honor a non-U.S. citizen, a precedent that apparently was not followed until some of the ballistic missile submarines were so named. She was paid for by the Philippine government, and manned for a time by a Filipino crew. A number of assigned names were switched between hull numbers prior to launching, evidently to suit local sentiment; but the reason for renaming *Ford* (DD-228), *John D. Ford* in 1921, almost a year after commissioning, is not clear.

Most of the flush deckers were completed too late to participate in the First World War, although some of the early ones got overseas before the armistice. While these saw little action, several suffered damage from accidents or groundings. The most serious of these mishaps overtook *Manley* on 19 March 1918 as she was escorting a convoy into port. While she was closing the British ship *Motagua* to deliver orders, the big liner somehow rolled down on *Manley's* depth charges. The resulting explosion blew off a good part of the destroyer's stern and ruptured gasoline and alcohol tanks, whose contents ran down into the crew's wrecked living spaces and burned for most of the night. Thirty British seamen and 34 Americans were killed, including *Manley's* executive officer, Lieutenant Commander Richard M. Elliot. The crippled destroyer was towed into Queenstown for repairs, and Commander Elliot was honored posthumously in the naming of *Manley's* near-sister, DD-146.

Such action as was seen by the others was mainly convoy escort and antisubmarine duty. Although no sinkings of German U-boats are attributed to the flush deckers in World War I, *Stringham* (DD-83) did almost as well by driving off *U-140* from an attempted attack on the Brazilian steamer *Uberaba* on 10 August 1918. For this good turn the grateful Brazilians presented their rescuer with a silk Ameri-

Caldwell (DD-69), first of the flush deckers, in dapple camouflage at Mare Island in 1917. Notice the open, canvas-covered bridge, location of the searchlight, and lack of antisubmarine weaponry. Ship is powerfully armed against surface opponents. The 3-inch antiaircraft gun is between the forecastle 4-inch gun and the bridge.

The Stockton as she appeared shortly after World War I. Open deckhouses amidships were common in the early flush deckers, but were later plated over. Galley was in amidships deckhouse, crew's head in after deckhouse. Soon after being recommissioned in 1940, this ship was transferred to Great Britain and served as HMS Ludlow.

can flag and a silver loving cup. During the war, the flush deckers also had their first experience with underwater listening gear when *Caldwell* worked for a while in 1918 with some experimental equipment. *Kane* (DD-235) was a belated war casualty when, on her first foreign cruise in October 1920, she exploded a mine in the Baltic Sea. Extensive damage to her hull, propellers, and shafting necessitated a pleasurable delay of six months in Swedish and British shipyards before she was able to join her sisters in the Mediterranean. *Brooks*, too, took a mine, off Riga, Latvia, toward the end of 1920. Temporarily repaired at the Burmeister and Wain yard in Copenhagen, she was taken in hand for thorough restoration by H. M. Dockyard at Chatham, England.

For others, there was the routine of occupation duty, such as keeping watch on the remnants of the Austro-Hungarian fleet at Spalato, Dalmatia. Postwar duty also saw many of the flush deckers in a variety of humanitarian roles. With famine and pestilence rampant throughout Eastern Europe and Asia Minor, it was natural that the fleet would be called in to assist the American relief agencies. *Biddle* (DD-151) was one of Rear Admiral Mark L. Bristol's helping hands in Turkish waters. Visiting nearly every port in the Black Sea and eastern Mediterranean, she shuttled loads of officials and relief cargo to places where they were needed, and lifted out refugees, the sick and wounded, and Americans caught in the mixed-up fighting between the Red and White armies in southern Russia. *Lawrence* (DD-250) did her bit and more, and with other destroyers of her detachment, evacuated thousands of Greek refugees fleeing from the areas of Asia Minor the Greek government had attempted unsuccessfully to wrest from the Turks. *Luce* (DD-99) not only covered the Adriatic, Aegean, and Black Sea, but pushed on up the Danube as well.

Overton (DD-239) put in one of the most interesting tours ever experienced by a destroyer. Under Commander Mark L. Bristol, Jr., she shuttled constantly about the troubled area: Gibraltar to Constantinople, Constanza, Batum, Yalta, Sevastopol, Samsun, Antalya, Messina, Haifa, Beirut, Alexandria, and many more, but never stayed more than a few days in any one port. She challenged mutinous Russian cruisers, intervened between the Greeks and the Turks, and was probably the only U. S. destroyer ever to run aground in the Danube River.

Launching of the Ward *(DD-139) on 1 June 1918, seventeen days after her keel was laid at the Mare Island Navy Yard. She was commissioned on 24 July. In 1922 she was decommissioned at San Diego and lay inactive until just before World War II. Photographs of other events in the* Ward's *life appear on pages 92 and 104.*

This happened 8 December 1920, at Galatz, Romania, when a storm drove her into the mud on the south bank of the river. Happily, she was able to extricate herself without difficulty. Her most publicized bit of relief work was the rescue of a 10-year old Armenian waif, a lad orphaned by war and massacre, who had been living inside the decayed hull of a beached fishing boat for over a year when *Overton's* crewmen noticed him near their anchorage in the Russian Black Sea port of Batum. The lad endeared himself to the ship's crew, and when they had to leave port they turned him over to their relief destroyer, where he became known as "Harry Overton." But Harry missed his old shipmates, and one day stowed away on a merchant vessel, by which eventually he got to Constantinople. When the *Overton* pulled into port, there, to the amazement of all hands, was Harry. After this, the ship all but let the boy move aboard as a crewman, took his education in hand, and even made strenuous efforts to have him adopted legally. One wonders where "Harry Overton" is today.

There was scarcely a ship in the U. S. Middle Eastern forces that did not show the flag on some errand of mercy. Probably the most spectacular rescue of all was carried out by *Bainbridge* (DD-246). On 16 December 1922, in the Sea of Marmara, she was passing the French military transport *Vinh-Long*, carrying dependents and ammunition from Bizerte to Constantinople, when the officer of the deck spotted a fire on the stern of the transport. Having pulled alongside, *Bainbridge* was twice blown away from the ill-fated ship by explosions. She finally managed to remain alongside by ramming her sharp bow into the flank of the burning Frenchman. Under these conditions the heroic destroyer crewmen succeeded in rescuing 482 of the 495 souls on board the doomed transport, and for this feat their commanding officer, Lieutenant Commander Walter A. Edwards, received the Medal of Honor.

Bainbridge's sister ships on the other side of the world were equally active. *Harding* (DD-91), in 1920, was drafted to rush bubonic plague antitoxin from New Orleans to Vera Cruz and Tampico, Mexico. As a result of this errand, she returned to a week of enforced quarantine and fumigation before being allowed to resume her normal duties. And in faraway Japan, after a violent earthquake had brought destruction to Tokyo and many smaller

cities in late August of 1923, flush deckers such as *Noa* (DD-343) and *John D. Edwards* (DD-216) appeared in Yokohama with food, medicine, and emergency assistance.

In the years following the First World War, many of the lower-numbered flush deckers were reduced to idleness at Philadelphia and San Diego, while the rest went to fill the Scouting and Battle Force squadrons of the peacetime Navy. For some, even getting completed was a struggle, as budgets were slashed and construction schedules slowed down while the country settled into the age of jazz, prohibition, and "normalcy." Many, like *Barry* (DD-248), were commissioned with a 50 per cent complement and held in reserve status for months before seeing active duty. Brave *Bainbridge* in similar conditions had no less than eight commanding officers in 1921, before shaking down to a more orderly pattern of existence. Some were relegated to menial chores. *Craven*, for example, was used in 1921, prior to decommissioning, to transport liberty parties between Charleston and Jacksonville. Twenty-four, laid up in 1922 after practically no real service, were destined to live in idleness until the scrapping torch ended their careers.

For others, life was glamorous. In addition to the normal battle problems and drills, there were European cruises to be made, ceremonies to be performed, and research projects to be carried out. Flush deckers escorted President Wilson on his trip to Versailles and met him when he returned home, frustrated and embittered. *Robinson* (DD-88) became particularly adept at honor escort duties, greeting both King Albert of Belgium and the Prince of Wales on their visits to the United States. *Corry* (DD-334) and *Hull* (DD-330) were with President Harding on his fatal trip to Alaska in August 1923. The following year, more happily, they sounded a route from Seattle to Seward for the new Alaskan cable. *Hull* performed other special assignments with her new sonic depth finder, sounding out to sea off the coast of southern California to a depth of 2,000 fathoms and locating several uncharted banks. *Converse* (DD-291), as an experimental ship, tested the Arma gyrocompass in 1921, the Flettner

rudder* in 1927, and various engineering and torpedo developments in 1928. There was scarcely a single event of naval interest during the 1920s in which flush deckers were not involved. Showing the flag in Mexico and the "Banana Republics," patrolling at international sailing races, making goodwill cruises to Australia and New Zealand, and protecting missionaries in revolution-torn China, were all a part of their day's work. When disaster struck other arms of the fleet, flush deckers were on the scene. *Overton* rushed volunteer workers to help in attempts to salvage the submarine *S-5*, sunk accidentally in 1920. *Mahan* (DM-7) assisted in salvage operations on both the *S-51* in 1925 and the *S-4* two years later.

But tragedy was always ready to strike at the flush deckers as well as at others. First of the class to go was *Woolsey* (DD-77), which on 26 February 1921 was rammed by the SS *Steel Inventor* and sunk off Panama in the first of a series of disasters that plagued the ships in the early 1920s. On 1 December of the same year, *De Long* (DD-129), operating under half complement, ran ashore in the fog at Half Moon Bay, California. Though subsequently salved and towed to Mare Island, she was decommissioned and scrapped soon thereafter. Scarcely two weeks later, on 16 December, *Graham* (DD-192) was rammed by the SS *Panama* off the New Jersey coast. Brought back into port, she was considered not worth repairing; instead, her bow was cut off and grafted onto *Hulbert* (DD-342) which had also been damaged in a collision, and the remainder of the ship was sold for scrap. But the most spectacular disaster was yet to come.

On Saturday, 8 September 1923, most of the ships of DesRon 11, Battle Fleet, were under way on a 24-hour test run from San Francisco to San Diego. *Delphy* (DD-261), carrying the squadron commander, was in the lead, followed by ComDesDiv 33 in *S. P. Lee* (DD-310), then *Young* (DD-312), *Woodbury* (DD-309), and *Nicholas* (DD-311) of his division; ComDesDiv 31 in *Farragut* (DD-300), with *Fuller* (DD-297), *Percival* (DD-298), *Somers* (DD-301), and *Chauncey* (DD-296) in column behind; and finally *Kennedy* (DD-306), *Paul Hamilton* (DD-307), *Stoddert* (DD-

First of 111 sisters, the Wickes, at anchor. In this peaceful scene, canvas shrouds her guns, depth charge racks, and galley deckhouse. Picture may have been taken during the period of the Rotating Reserve, 1932-1934, when one crew tried to keep two ships going.

The disposition of the guns and torpedo tubes and the layout of the upper works are plain in this aerial view of the Lamson (DD-328) taken sometime between her commissioning in September 1920 and October 1927 when the photograph was printed in the U. S. Naval Institute Proceedings.

---

* The Flettner rudder was intended to eliminate the need for a steering engine by making manual control easier. It consisted of three vertical blades, resembling an ordinary rudder with extra blades connected to either side by struts. On the center blade was a small auxiliary rudder like a trim tab on a modern airplane. This, when turned manually, caused the main blades to follow suit. The device did not work well at low speeds and was soon discarded by the Navy, although it was used in modified form on merchant ships for some time.

302), and *Thompson* (DD-305) of Division 32. That night the flagship broadcast her 2000 position report showing the squadron about nine miles off Point Arguello, and an hour later turned abruptly eastward on a course to enter Santa Barbara Channel. Unknown to the destroyermen, the ships had been set considerably in toward land, possibly by abnormal currents resulting from the great Tokyo earthquake of the preceding week. An improperly interpreted radio compass bearing was the final link in a chain of events that led to disaster. As the ships swung left into their turn, those in the rear could see the leader disappear into the thick bank of fog which, as usual, blanketed the California coast. Each succeeding destroyer followed in the leader's wake. Not five minutes later *Delphy*, at 20 knots, struck with a terrible grating on the rocks of Pedernales Point, near Honda, just north of Point Arguello. Then *S. P. Lee* hit and swung broadside against the bluffs of the mainland, while *Young*, piling up alongside *Delphy*, was flipped over on her side by the latter's propeller wash in less than two minutes. *Woodbury* came to grief on a rocky islet just offshore; *Nicholas* was on the reefs to seaward of *Lee*; and *Fuller* was aground out beyond *Woodbury*. Finally, *Chauncey* sliced in close beside capsized *Young*, while *Somers* and *Farragut*, warned in the nick of time by the flagship's shrieking siren, had slowed down sufficiently to enable them to back off after touching ground. The other five avoided grounding altogether. In the chaos that followed, crewmen of the stranded but otherwise intact ships started rescue work on behalf of their less fortunate comrades. Survivors of the *Young* made their way over a life line to *Chauncey*, while fishing boats summoned by *Somers* and the others milling about offshore plucked stranded sailors from *Woodbury* and *Fuller*. The rest got ashore by life line or by jumping onto the rocks and wading through the surf. Some had to stick it out on the pounding wrecks until morning, and it was not until Sunday afternoon that the last survivor had been rescued. In the final count, 23 men were lost, most of them from the nearly sunken *Young*. As the drenched survivors came ashore, they were rounded up and sheltered in an improvised camp set up by local ranchers awakened by *Delphy's* siren, and taken to San Diego by special train within a few hours. Their ships became total losses. In 1925 their wreckage was sold to a hopeful salvager for a mere 1,035 dollars.

The Hovey *slices cleanly through a calm sea in 1932, torpedo tubes trained out for a practice attack.* Hovey *and* Long *carried eight 4-inch in twin mounts. Note small sponson in way of after 4-inch mount on main deck, 3-inch gun on after deckhouse, absence of depth charge racks. For a short time,* Stockton *(DD-73) carried a twin 4-inch on her forecastle.*

Another especially heavily armed flush decker was Hatfield, *with four 5-inch, seen leaving New York for duty in Spanish waters, 17 August 1936. Just as in the* Hovey, *her aftermost main battery mount is on the main deck, and her anti-aircraft weapon is on the deckhouse. Four sisters were identically armed:* Brooks, Gilmer, Fox, *and* Kane. Hatfield *was the last of the four-stack flush deckers to be stricken from the Navy List, in 1947.*

Childs (DD-241) became another casualty on 4 April 1929, when she rammed and sank the schooner *A. Ernest Mills* off the Virginia Capes, losing a good bit of her bow in the process. The Norfolk Navy Yard got the job of fabricating a new one for her.

A special feature in the early careers of several of the destroyers was duty with the infant naval aviation arm. The flush deckers enjoyed a close and continuing affiliation with the aviators. *Harding* (DD-91) started in May 1919, accompanying the rest of her division, to guide Seaplane Division One under Commander John H. Towers on the Navy Seaplane Trans-Atlantic Flight. The destroyers stationed themselves at intervals from Newfoundland all the way to the Azores, pouring smoke from their funnels by day and beaming their searchlights or firing star shells by night. As the seaplanes passed overhead, the destroyers would pick up speed and follow them toward the next port. Only a few miles short of the Azores, *NC-1* and *NC-3* were forced to the water in a dense fog. *NC-1* had already been abandoned by her crew when *Harding*, answering the plane's SOS, arrived on the scene. The destroyermen soon had a working party alongside the derelict aircraft, and struggled for five hours to save it, only to be driven off by rising seas that caused the hulk to capsize and go down. *Harding* then proceeded to stand by the downed *NC-3*, whose gallant crew, refusing all assistance, taxied their plane into port. Next, she was on hand to greet the successful *NC-4* when it flew in to alight at Ponta Delgada in the Azores on 20 May 1919; then she hurried on to El Ferrol, Spain, to meet the plane again and entertain and berth its crew.

After her return to the States and a brief period in reduced commission, *Harding*, along with the *Mugford* (DD-105), was prepared for duty as a tender to seaplane divisions, chiefly through the replacement of her after tubes with gasoline tanks, and was based at Pensacola under the operational control of Commander Air Detachment, U. S. Atlantic Fleet. At that time, Pensacola was already the Navy's largest training center for both lighter-than-air and heavier-than-air instruction. On 30 July 1920 six aviation officers, including one Lieutenant Felix B. Stump (later CinCPacFlt), reported aboard the *Harding* for training in the *NC-7* and *NC-8*. Aviation duties took the ship to Jacksonville, Key West, and around the Caribbean by way of Guantanamo Bay, Old Providence Island, the Canal

Zone, Honduras, Mexico, Haiti, and back to Florida. After some shipyard alterations, *Harding* operated out of Hampton Roads in connection with the practice bombing of ex-German prizes and superannuated U. S. battleships by the Army Air Service under General Billy Mitchell. On 21 July 1921, she was on the scene when the Army bombers jumped the gun and sank the ex-German battleship *Ostfriesland* with two 1,000-pound bomb hits, while the minelayer USS *Shawmut* was still within the danger circle. It was from these early tests that naval aviation received the impetus that led to the development of the big carriers, but *Harding's* part ended the next day. After a few routine operations, she headed for inactivation and oblivion.

The next flush decker to assume a particularly intimate connection with air operations was *Charles Ausburn* (DD-294). Standard duties occupied her until August 1923 when she received a seaplane from Naval Air Station, Norfolk. The plane was a TS-1, one of the first types designed especially for shipboard operations and equipped with what may have been the first of the radial engines, the Lawrence J-1. A working party from the pioneer carrier *Langley* and the naval air station came aboard and fixed up a cradle for the plane, whereupon the destroyer got under way for experimental operations with the Scouting Fleet along the Atlantic coast. The objective was to determine the feasibility of carrying scouting aircraft on destroyers, as had already been authorized for battleships, cruisers, and even (in one instance) submarines. *Charles Ausburn* demonstrated that this was possible, but recommended that any planes carried on destroyers thereafter be located on the quarterdeck because of interferences on the forecastle. Although nothing significant seems to have come of these early experiments, *Charles Ausburn* appears to have had the distinction of being the first destroyer to carry her own airplane. Continuing her association with the aeronauts, she was one of many flush deckers to serve as a station ship for the U. S. Army Round-the-World Flight of 1924; her post was off Greenland. This four-plane flight was made from west to east, and among those standing guard along the route across the Pacific was *Noa* (DD-343), a ship that was to pick up the thread of air operations in 1939.

As the fleet settled down to the routine of the 1920s, things were relatively quiet until 1929 when

the Secretary of the Navy included the following in his annual report:

"Due to age and continuous service for 10 years, the material condition of the destroyers in active service indicates that those having Yarrow boilers (60 in commission) have reached the end of their useful life and must be replaced. . . . The department does not consider that the large expenditure which would be necessary to place these old destroyers in good condition is justified. Consequently, they will be decommissioned with the view of their ultimate removal from the Navy list."

These dry words concealed an appalling situation. The impact of the loss of 60 active destroyers (out of 103 in commission plus six DMs) under any circumstances would have been bad enough, but in 1929 no funds were budgeted for more than normal upkeep expenses. The entire job of refitting replacements for the worn-out destroyers had to be undertaken by the Fleet itself. Its accomplishment, begun officially on 17 September 1929, was reported by one of the participants, Lieutenant Commander D. P. Moon, in the article "Recommissioning the Destroyers," in the *U. S. Naval Institute Proceedings* for February 1931: "For nearly a year all normal operations and training of these squadrons ceased. In the place of such operations was substituted the functions of a seagoing navy yard in modernizing and recommissioning . . . destroyers in reserve." As finally worked out, the plan involved replacing the 11th and 12th Squadrons of the Battle Fleet and the 9th Squadron of the Scouting Fleet with the 6th, 10th, and 7th Reserve Squadrons, respectively. When the switch was at its height, only eight destroyers were in commission in the Pacific. The squadron commanders examined all the reserve destroyers to select those most suitable for recommissioning. The instructions finally issued "involved the shifting of masts, bridges in whole or in part, searchlight towers, radio installations, gyros, gun carriages and slides, torpedo tubes, torpedo and fire-control equipment, and pumps from the old destroyers to the new ones. . . . the orders called for the wiring of torpedo and fire-control systems, the installation of ship's wiring, the installation of voice tubing, the retubing of condensers when required, the rearranging of magazines, the lifting of turbine casings, and finally the overhaul and conditioning of all machinery in addition to all the construction and repair alterations."

Harding shows her affiliation with naval aviation by the star on her first funnel and the gasoline tanks in place of her after tubes. Photo, taken in 1920, shows unshaded bow numbers, open galley deckhouse, tall mainmast, and searchlight platform on after deckhouse.

Truxtun and Sharkey (DD-281) differed from their sisters in carrying a patent anchor instead of the old-fashioned type which rested on a billboard on the forecastle.

A small seaplane was mounted on a platform forward of the bridge on Charles Ausburn in 1923. The single-seat aircraft belonged to Observation Squadron One.

On experimental duty in 1927, the Osborne carries a temporary deckhouse abaft the fourth stack, and has all her torpedo tubes removed. A few years later she was stricken and converted to a banana freighter, under the Honduran flag.

In September, at the Destroyer Base in San Diego, base personnel, the tenders *Melville* and *Altair*, the cruiser *Omaha*, and repair ship *Medusa*, the last-named borrowed from the battleships, all pitched into the job. Each destroyer to be discarded was assigned a mate, which she towed out of "red lead row" to a berth alongside a buoy or tender. Similar events took place in Philadelphia with the Atlantic ships. It was an unprecedented undertaking, and unmatched in the later history of the Navy. "The unfavorable impressions of the reserve ships later proved to be largely unwarranted. . . . there was but little corrosion within. Below decks, the ships were clean and dry and in an excellent state of preservation . . . pans of unslaked lime in the compartments, renewed at intervals, had removed moisture from the air and retarded corrosive action, but much of the preservative employed in the machinery required many hours of labor to remove." The great do-it-yourself job showed excellent results —the first of the revitalized destroyers was recommissioned 8 January 1930, and the last on 4 June— all accomplished by forces afloat, with a minimum of shipyard help.

Now that the second team, so to speak, had taken the field, 58 of the worn-out ships went to their doom on various scrap piles or were otherwise discarded in accordance with the terms of the 1930 London Treaty on Naval Limitations. Before being sold for scrap, *Preston* (DD-327) and *Bruce* (DD-329) made a final contribution by having their hulls propped up on blocks in the Norfolk Navy Yard dry dock and deliberately buckled; one by hogging (that is, supported in the middle and weighted down at both ends), and the other by sagging, to determine under controlled conditions just how much strain the ships could take. These tests demonstrated conclusively the superiority of the longitudinal method of framing over the transverse method used in the construction of the flush deckers. The results were applied directly in the building of the new *Farragut* class (DD-348 through 355), the first U.S. destroyers laid down after World War I. In transverse framing, the main strength members are the ribs or athwartship frames, to which the side plating is attached. In the longitudinal method, the hull is designed as a girder. It results in a better-balanced design, in which the strength is approximately the same against all modes of failure. Transverse-framed

ships were more likely to break in two from underwater damage. *Moody* (DD-277), sold to Metro-Goldwyn-Mayer for 5,000 dollars, was starred in a movie called "Sea Pigs," in the course of which she was sunk to make the battle scenes realistic, 1933-style.

The economy-minded and depression-ridden year of 1930 saw the start of the major efforts toward putting the flush deckers to new uses, but to pick up the real beginnings of the conversion program it is necessary to backtrack to 1919. The lessons of the Great War had demonstrated the value of fast ships capable of laying offensive minefields, and in 1920-21, 14 of the flush-deck destroyers had their torpedo tubes removed, and mine tracks with a capacity of 80 mines (in some cases more) were installed in their place. Redesignated Light Mine-layers in 1920, for the most part they still carried their DD hull numbers, but also had the Mine Force insignia painted on their bows. In 1930, six of the original DMs were scrapped and four additional conversions authorized. Again, in 1936-37, when the remainder of the first batch were scrapped, their places were taken by four new conversions. Thus, eight DMs were on hand to enter World War II. After 1938 they wore DM numbers on their bows.

The year 1930 also saw the start of a development that was to provide many a lurid feature story for the Sunday supplements and popular scientific magazines under such headings as "Ghost Fleet of the Pacific." On 1 August 1930, the Chief of Naval Operations announced the intention of installing radio control on three destroyers, *Stoddert* (DD-302), *Hazelwood* (DD-107), and *Sinclair* (DD-275), which were redesignated Light Target numbers 1, 2, and 3 (IX-35, 36, and 37), respectively. On 25 August, Lieutenant Commander Boyd R. Alexander took command of the "radio-controlled High Speed Destroyer Target Unit," consisting of *Stoddert* in "operating, but decommissioned status," which he was under orders to transfer from San Diego to Mare Island under her own power with a pick-up skeleton crew. Her overhaul and conversion at that yard were estimated to cost just under 10,000 dollars, a figure achieved only by dint of wholesale salvage, cannibalization, and do-it-yourself work on the part of ship's force. *Stoddert*, after demonstrating the feasibility of radio control in a most satisfactory manner, was replaced by *Lamberton*

The **Hart** *(DM-8) anchored in a Chinese river when she was with the Asiatic Fleet. Built as DD-110, she was redesignated a light mine-layer in 1920 and her torpedo tubes were replaced by mine tracks with a reported capacity of 80 mines.*

In 1931 the Hart was stricken and sold. Her most valuable parts were taken for scrap and the remainder was sunk for use as a breakwater at a seaplane base at Alameda, California, in company with several other old destroyers. Photograph by courtesy of Ted Stone.

(DD-119) in 1932. The cases of the other light targets were somewhat confused. The ships originally designated were among those enmeshed in the boiler defect, economy, and disarmament problems of the early 1930s. *Hazelwood's* designation was cancelled and *Boggs* (DD-136) became Light Target Number 2. Number 3 remained stillborn. *Sinclair's* designation was cancelled in favor of *Kilty* (DD-137), and *Kilty's* in favor of *Radford* (DD-120). These ships were assigned various IX and AG classification numbers, but never did see service as targets. *Lamberton* and *Boggs*, however, together with the disarmed ex-battleship *Utah*, and destroyers *Dorsey* (DD-117) and *Elliot* (DD-146) as control ships, made up Mobile Target Division One (MoTarDiv) of the Base Force, U. S. Fleet. Although their employment was strictly in the role of targets for gunfire and air bombing (actually, the firing was done at target rafts towed astern), where they could be made to change course and speed on radio command from a control ship or plane, the imagination of many a writer was fired with visions of a ghostly unmanned fleet, stealing up to ram the enemy or blast him with crewless guns and robot torpedoes. Needless to say, such developments never came to pass. As an example of what the MoTars actually could do, *Lamberton's* skipper gave the following estimate of her operational capabilities: continuous operation for ten hours at 29 knots or 24 hours at 24 knots; a three-and-one-half-hour period required for warm-up, final test, and shifting of personnel to the control ship before starting a run; and an average of one hour's servicing after every four hours of remote operation. *Stoddert* was scrapped in 1935, but the other mobile targets stayed on to be converted back to fighting roles when World War II provided the fleet with an adequate supply of enemy-manned mobile targets.

Between 1930 and 1932, six of the flush deckers were mustered into the Coast Guard. With torpedo tubes and some guns removed, they joined a number of older destroyers chasing speedy rumrunners and otherwise aiding in the effort to enforce prohibition. These ships were returned to the Navy in mid-1934 when, with one exception, they went out of commission.

Semmes (DD-189), the exception, was designated to relieve *Eagle 58* as an underwater sound experimental ship. The Philadelphia Navy Yard converted her to specifications drawn up by the Naval Research Laboratory, installing four sonar hoists and sea chests, altering the forward magazine and adjacent fuel tanks into a sound room, and installing the special equipment removed from *Eagle 58*. The crew of the old Eagle Boat thereupon moved aboard *Semmes* and recommissioned her as AG-24, under which designation she served in Experimental Division One at the Submarine Base, New London, and elsewhere for many years. She was responsible for checking out most of the advances in underwater acoustic technology which led to our World War II sonar equipment, and she participated in a few wild-goose chases as well, such as a 1936 project to use underwater sound to explode depth charges and mines.

Although the 1930s saw the beginning of the unrest that developed into World War II, they marked the low period of the flush deckers. From 1932 to 1934 there was little activity to be seen. Duties were routine. In many cases, in order to keep ships in service it was necessary to resort to such drastic expedients as reduced commission and the Rotating Reserve, in which one crew tried to keep two ships going by alternating a few months at a time on each. Casualties were few during this period, but *Sicard* (DD-346) was rammed by *Lea* (DD-118) off Oahu, on 12 May 1935, suffering considerable damage. On 14 April 1936, *Smith Thompson* (DD-212) was rammed by *Whipple* (DD-217) in Philippine waters and was so badly damaged that when she was finally towed into Subic Bay she was deemed not worth the expense of repairing. Consequently, *Smith Thompson* was decommissioned far from home and her hulk towed outside the bay and sunk in deep water on 25 July 1936.

In the mid-1930s, under the requirements of the London Treaty, 35 more flush deckers were culled out of the reserve fleets and sacrificed on the altar of disarmament. Most of this group had served only three or four years in commission, and many a tear must have been shed in helpless frustration scarcely three years later when the demands of war made ships of their class of inestimable value. But, with three exceptions, they were gone forever, broken up, and their scrap, as likely as not, sold to the booming steel mills of Japan. For *Taylor* (DD-94), *Walker* (DD-163), and *Turner* (DD-259), the cry of war sounded just in time to stay the auctioneer's hammer in its final fall, and their hulls sur-

The first mobile target, Stoddert, *makes high speed under radio control. She flies two black balls to indicate that she is not under command. The tin hats on her funnels were intended to protect the boilers from bomb damage. Though designated IX-35, she still wears her destroyer number.*

U.S. Coast Guard Destroyer Hunt *(CG-18) was one of five flush deckers to serve in the rum patrol from 1930 to 1934. The others were* Abel P. Upshur *(CG-15),* George E. Badger *(CG-16),* Herndon *(CG-17),* Welborn C. Wood *(CG-19), and* Semmes *(CG-20). The Coast Guard, needing neither torpedo tubes nor the after 4-inch gun, had them removed and stored ashore.*

vived to contribute, albeit unconventionally, to the war effort.

The only duty that offered much out of the ordinary for any length of time was the Special Service Squadron, which was kept moderately busy by the repetitious revolutions of the Central American and Caribbean countries. The year 1936 saw civil war break out in Spain, a conflict which, as is now recognized, was a dress rehearsal by the Axis dictators for World War II. The Navy organized a small force, Squadron 40T, including several of the flush deckers, to evacuate American citizens and to keep an eye on things. *Kane* (DD-235), of this group, was near-missed by six bombs from an unidentified plane off Bilbao, on 30 August 1936, but suffered no damage. Neither did the plane, although the destroyer returned two rounds from her 3-inch/23 antiaircraft gun. The squadron was disbanded in October 1940 because of more pressing international developments.

Gilmer (DD-233), between 1931 and 1935, evaluated for destroyer use the 5-inch/25, which was the standard antiaircraft gun for battleships and cruisers until it was superseded by the dual-purpose 5-inch/38 and the 3-inch/50. Unnoticed behind a veil of security, the first American search radar went to sea in *Leary* (DD-158) in April 1937. So stringent was the secrecy imposed on this development that it was years before the word "radar" could even be used in public.

Another destroyer that entered experimental service was *Dahlgren* (DD-187). Selected to become an engineering test ship, she entered New York Navy Yard in 1937 for the installation of a new high-temperature, high-pressure power plant. The two boilers in her after fire room were replaced by Babcock and Wilcox "Steamotive" boilers operating at 1,300 p.s.i. and 910 degrees F., and her two after stacks were trunked into a single broad funnel. The old propulsion machinery was stripped out and new General Electric geared turbines installed in the forward engine room. The Bureau of Construction and Repair even authorized the cutting of a door in the bulkhead between the forward engine and fire rooms to facilitate access during test and evaluation of the new plant, probably making her the only destroyer in which it was not necessary to go "up and over" to pass between those spaces!

Flush deckers rejoined the naval aviation service in 1938 when *Childs* (DD-241) and *Williamson*

(DD-244) entered Philadelphia Navy Yard to be converted to small seaplane tenders (AVP). The alterations consisted of removing the forward boilers and two stacks, all torpedo tubes, and all but two guns; and adding fuel tanks, workshops, living spaces, storerooms, and equipment to support a squadron of 12 PBY-type seaplanes and their crews. Completion of the work was urgently desired by January 1939, to permit evaluation of the ships during the fleet problem scheduled for that year. So successful were they that seven destroyers in all were assigned to this use and redesignated AVP-14 through 20. In 1940 these ships were reclassified AVD to distinguish them from the other classes of AVP, and seven more were converted and recommissioned from the inactive destroyer list.

An aviation experiment of a different type was carried out on *Noa*. Fitted with a seaplane which nested just forward of the after deckhouse (replacing the after torpedo tubes), and a boom for lifting it aboard, she departed in May 1940 for tests off the Delaware Capes, in which an XSOC-1 seaplane, piloted by Lieutenant G. L. Heap, was hoisted onto the ocean for takeoff and recovered by the ship while she was under way. On 15 May, Lieutenant Heap made an emergency flight to transfer a sick man to the Naval Hospital at Philadelphia. These dramatic demonstrations convinced the Secretary of the Navy of the value of destroyer-based scout planes, and on the twenty-seventh of that same month he directed that six new destroyers of the soon-to-be-built *Fletcher* class (DD-476-481) be fitted with catapults and handling equipment. Shortcomings in the hoisting gear led to the cancellation of this program in early 1943. Thus this concept failed to mature as a combat technique, and *Noa* spent most of her time on experimental work, and training midshipmen out of Annapolis. The destroyer-observation seaplane team, although it had failed to materialize on *Charles Ausburn* and again on *Noa*, was to be revived under somewhat modified conditions during amphibious operations late in the war.

A second four stacker shorn down to three in this immediately prewar period was *Hamilton* (DD-141), altered by the New York Navy Yard in late 1939 to test gyroscopes and stabilizing systems. For this purpose the forward boiler was replaced with stabilization tanks connected by a cross channel through which water was pumped from side to side

Three stages in the life of a destroyer. Top view shows the Dahlgren at Guantanamo Bay soon after she was commissioned in 1920. Idle from 1922 to 1932, she was broken out of retirement and operated with the Fleet for five years.

In 1937 the Dahlgren had new boilers and turbines fitted in place of the old ones. The third and fourth funnels were trunked, torpedo tubes removed, and new deckhouses cluttered her silhouette. Photograph by courtesy of Our Navy magazine.

During the war Dahlgren sprouted radar, a large number of light antiaircraft guns, and several K guns to supplement the depth charge racks aft. Half her torpedo battery was remounted. She served as an escort, patrol vessel, and sonar school ship.

by a hydraulic oscillator unit. In addition, a portable deckhouse was fitted to carry the gyroscopes being tested. In still-water trials, activation of the stabilizing system would make the destroyer roll as much as 18 degrees, and previous model tests indicated that the equipment should have been able to counteract seas which ordinarily would cause a 30-degree roll. However, difficulties were encountered and before they could be corrected, war had broken out in Europe. Experimental work came to a halt as the Navy prepared for combat. *Hamilton's* gear was removed, and in 1941 she was converted to a high-speed minesweeper. (As a postscript to this experiment, the stabilization equipment was stored for almost a decade, until interest was revived in 1948. In order to use as much as possible of the special equipment, testing was resumed on the 221-foot minesweeper *Peregrine*, since the displacement and natural period of roll of that ship were similar to *Hamilton's*, and a 30 per cent improvement in stabilization was recorded.)

With the obvious approach of war in Europe, the rest of the flush deckers began to be hauled out of the backwaters where some of them had been languishing since 1922. During early 1939, in anticipation of hostilities, the Board of Inspection and Survey was given the task of making a thorough scrutiny of the reserve destroyers, in the course of which it made some interesting observations, such as these taken from a report on the San Diego group:

"Compared to conditions existing in the past, the material condition of the vessels inspected indicates that the methods which have been developed are proving more effective. . . . the material condition of the decommissioned DDs is directly affected by the degree of thoroughness with which the vessels were decommissioned. There are many examples on the vessels decommissioned in 1922 and 1923 indicating that the lack of thoroughness has resulted in serious deterioration of material. . . . improvement of conditions is largely due to the vigilance and standards of thoroughness established by the present C. O., Capt. Byron McCandless, USN, and his senior assistants. . . . While the advent of war is indeterminate, the fact exists that we are nearer that event than when the destroyers were first decommissioned. . . ."

The methods established by Captain McCandless were based on a two-stage overhaul procedure; in the first cycle, the goal was "practical" perfection;

in the second, "actual" perfection. After overhaul, each ship was expected to be ready for recommissioning, except for alterations and major repairs requiring shipyard work. Because of money restrictions, Captain McCandless and his crews could only itemize these work orders in detail, so that the ships would be ready for work to start on the overhauls whenever the word would be given. As an indication of the extent to which such work had accumulated on some of the ships, there was the problem of some winches that were found on the sterns of *Kilty* (DD-137) and *Kennison* (DD-138). After voluminous correspondence with all the material bureaus and the Chief of Naval Operations, it was finally ascertained that the winches had been installed back in 1919 to secure kite balloons, which at that time were favored as a means of antiaircraft defense. The winches were removed but thriftily saved for future use, and they undoubtedly turned up in some unexpected place to help win the next war. The Board of Inspection and Survey concluded its report with a recommendation that the "material bureaus should consider without delay the type of replacement equipment to be used in the event of war and that where the present equipment is obviously obsolete, it should be removed now. The degree of confusion that will undoubtedly exist during mobilization will be so great as to justify all reasonable advance preparations." To which one can only add "Amen."

These forehanded preparations proved their value in the "destroyers for bases" swap of 1940, when 50 of the recommissioned ships were turned over to the British and Canadians. They became known as the "Town" class because practically all were renamed after towns common to both the United States and the United Kingdom. So near had some of these ships come to the grave that their names had been taken away and given to new destroyers. Thus DD-70 and DD-185 had to be renamed *Conway* and *Doran*, respectively, which has caused confusion to this day among old-timers who knew the ships when they were *Craven* and *Bagley*, and who knew equally well that there had never been any flush deckers named *Conway* and *Doran!* Despite the long years of inactivity, no effort was spared to return the destroyers to first-class condition, as is indicated in a description penned by Captain Taprell Dorling, DSO, RN ("Taffrail").

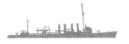

Childs, the first destroyer seaplane tender, wearing her AVP designator in the Delaware River in April 1939. Just a year later all the flush-deck AVPs were given new numbers in the AVD series, and Childs became AVD-1. Another photograph of this ship appears on page 44.

The Noa at the Philadelphia Navy Yard in 1939, showing her scout plane rig. A sturdy crane was stepped in place of the mainmast. The single-float, two-place seaplane was borrowed from Cruiser Scouting Squadron Three. In 1940 Noa had two aircraft assigned.

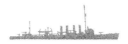

"The ships had been refitted throughout. They were scrupulously clean and fully supplied. Complete outfits of ammunition and other warlike equipment were left on board, together with stores of all kinds. Everything was handed over to the new owners—paint and cordage; messtraps, silver and china, all marked with the anchor and U.S.N.; towels, sheets, blankets, mattresses and pillows. Sextant, chronometer watch, high-powered binoculars for the use of officers and look-outs, parallel rulers and instruments for navigation were not forgotten. A typewriter, paper, envelopes, patent pencil sharpeners, pencils, ink—everything and anything one could imagine, even to books and magazines, an electric coffee machine in the wardroom, were all provided. Storerooms were fully stocked with provisions, including spiced tinned ham and tinned sausages, and canned fruit and corn which do not normally find a place in the dietary of British blue-jackets."

More significant than the British amazement over tinned corn and patent pencil sharpeners was the hard fact of Britain's desperate need for these ships. Prime Minister Churchill, speaking to the House of Commons on 5 November 1940, declared: "The 50 American destroyers are rapidly coming into service just when they are most needed." And Admiral of the Fleet Sir James Somerville wrote even more strongly: "Had there been no American 'four stacker' destroyers available and had they not gone into service escorting trade convoys when they did, the outcome of the struggle against the U-boat and the subsequent outcome of the European War itself might have been vastly different."

The renaming of the destroyers by the British produced some interesting duplication of names held by others of their sisters, such as:

USS Ludlow (DD-112)
  HMS Ludlow (ex DD-73)
USS Montgomery (DD-121)
  HMS Montgomery (ex DD-75)
USS Caldwell (DD-69)
  HMS Caldwell (ex DD-133)
USS Hamilton (DD-141)
  HMS Hamilton (ex DD-170)
USS Ramsay (DD-124)
  HMS Ramsey (ex DD-274)

A variation on this theme developed when USS Tillman (DD-135) became HMS Wells. USS Welles (DD-257), in turn, became HMS Cameron.

The history of these 50 ships is a fascinating study in itself. Some indication of the rough service they encountered may be gleaned from the bare statistics: they were involved in 15 serious collisions, four instances of major gale damage, and four ground-ings; ten were sunk, and six others severely dam-aged by enemy action; at one time or another, 16 served with the Royal Canadian Navy, five with the Royal Norwegian Navy, one with the Polish Navy, and nine under the red star of the USSR, in whose service one was sunk. The record for service under various flags was held by Lincoln (ex-Yarnall, DD-143), which at different stages in the war, did duty with the British, the Norwegians, the Canadians, and the Russians.

The destroyers were delivered by U. S. naval steaming crews to Halifax, where they were re-ceived by their British crews and commissioned after a day or two of familiarization. The British were rather hard put to find crews for so many ships at once, and at their urging the Canadians agreed to take first four, then two more of them. Five of these six (Annapolis was the exception) were named, not after towns as were the rest of the class, but after rivers common to the United States and Canada. Columbia (ex-Haraden) was almost exchanged back to the Royal Navy because her engines and boilers were different from the other five Canadian ships, and it was thought this might cause a logistic problem; but she was kept anyway rather than wait for another ship to arrive. A seventh ship, Hamilton, got involved in a collision with sister ship Georgetown. After repairs had been made, she grounded while undocking at St. John, New Brunswick, and suffered so much more damage that an extended refit was required. Her crew was transferred to another destroyer and she was taken over by a Canadian care and maintenance party, then commissioned in the Canadian Navy in June 1941. The British ships departed in five flotillas between September and November 1940, and while crews were still being assembled for the last group, a number of the ships were maintained by Canadian shipkeepers.

The effect of heavy armament on a narrow, shallow-draft hull was to make the British doubt that the flush deckers were stable enough for winter operations in the North Atlantic. Furthermore, their torpedo and single-purpose gun armament was not designed for antisubmarine or antiaircraft work.

Accordingly, the Admiralty, which is notably conservative in matters of weight and stability, immediately made a number of alterations, including shortening the foremast and removing its searchlight platform, replacing the mainmast with a short stump to support the radio antennas, and removing the two after sets of torpedo tubes and one of the motor boats. To improve the ASW capability of the ships, a tactical range recorder was added to their sonar, which made it more compatible with the British Asdic. During successive refits, five feet were cut off the after three stacks; radar was installed; the 3-inch AA gun replaced with a 12-pounder; wing 4-inch mounts replaced with 20mm. Oerlikon machine guns and more of these added; torpedo armament further reduced to a single centerline mount; boat davits lowered and relocated; bridges closed in and given a "squared off" appearance; and the interior made more habitable (by British standards) by replacing the bouncy, inner-spring mattresses in the officers' bunks with thin hair mattresses. Several received escort modifications in which all torpedo tubes and 4-inch guns were removed and light antiaircraft guns mounted in their stead. *Bradford*, *Stanley*, and *Clare* had a complete rebuilding to become long-range escorts, losing their two forward funnels and boilers, as did those the United States converted to seaplane tenders, to gain perhaps 20 per cent additional fuel capacity and endurance. In 1943, many of the remaining "Town" class ships had their aftermost stack and boiler removed for the same reason. Toward the end of their service some were modernized to the extent of mounting a Hedgehog antisubmarine mortar in place of the bow gun.

Service under the White Ensign had its surprises for the old destroyers. *Ludlow*, with a heavy Gaelic element in her crew, was customarily played in and out of harbor by a Scottish piper. On the more sombre side, casualties were not long in coming. *Cameron*, while undergoing her initial alterations, was caught in dry dock at Portsmouth, England, by German bombers during the blitz—5 December 1940—and bombed right off her blocks. Her wrecked hull made an unusual contribution to the U. S. Navy when experts from America swarmed over it, gauging the extent of damage and calculating measures to improve damage control in her sisters. Because of the circumstances which permitted close review of such serious damage, her case became rather celebrated in naval construction

circles, and she was considered to represent the worst case of destroyer damage until the USS *Cassin* (DD-372) and *Downes* (DD-375) were almost completely destroyed in dry dock at Pearl Harbor. *Cameron* was salvaged, but she was too badly racked to be fit for further sea duty, and was used as a hulk for shock tests for the rest of the war.

Having been put right to work escorting convoys and chasing subs, the British flush deckers were soon in on their first kill. In an unprecedented action, *Niagara* boarded *U-570*, 28 August 1941, after the submarine had surrendered to an airplane of the Royal Air Force. Brought safely to port, the U-boat was recommissioned in the Royal Navy as HMS *Graph*. This victory was some consolation for the blood which the German submariners had drawn just a few days before. *Bath*, sailing under the Norwegian flag, was torpedoed and sunk 19 August 1941. She was followed by *Broadwater* on 18 October, *Stanley* on 19 December, and *Belmont* on 31 January 1942. *Campbeltown*, disguised as a German *Möwe* class destroyer with two rakish stacks, immolated herself by ramming at 20 knots into the lock gate at St. Nazaire. Her forecastle was packed with almost five tons of depth charges cemented into a steel and concrete tank. This self-propelled time bomb blew up two and one-half hours after the British commando force withdrew from its great raid on the Nazi-held port, 28 March 1942, taking with it to oblivion a large German inspection party which was swarming over the "captured" Trojan horse. More important, the explosion ruined the only dry dock on the French coast capable of taking the German battleship *Tirpitz*.

On 2 May 1942, *St. Albans* sank a submarine, but tragically it turned out to be the Polish *Jastrzab* (Falcon), formerly the USS *S-25* which had recently been turned over to the British. Pugnacious *Churchill*, patrolling off the Venezuelan coast one night in June of that year, sighted a low-lying target which she promptly fired at and attempted to ram. A last-minute swerving of course saved her by about six yards from hitting the islet of La Sola!

The next month was marked by *St. Croix* sinking the *U-90*. At the North African landings in November 1942, *Clare*, doing her part at Algiers, was the only British flush decker represented. The others were fighting the North Atlantic winter as well as the Germans. At least, most of them were. *Churchill* happened to be enjoying a three-month overhaul at

Charleston, South Carolina, where her sailors spent their leave living and working on farms in the surrounding countryside and entertaining themselves on liberty in town every night.

The winter of 1942-43 brought some of the worst weather in the memory of old-time Newfoundlanders. Gales of hurricane force put the seaworthiness of the flush-deck destroyers to a grim test. *Beverley* fought her way into St. John's with only five tons of fuel oil left in her tanks, while *Caldwell*, her bridge stove in and engines damaged, ran out of fuel completely, and was believed lost while she wallowed helplessly in the storm. When finally found and towed into port, she was discovered to be damaged beyond the capacity of the local repair facilities, so her screws were removed to facilitate towing and she was hauled off toward Boston. Two days out, another storm broke the tow and forced the tug to seek shelter. Other tugs sent to rescue the helpless hulk were driven back by high seas and heavy icing. Sister ship HMCS *Columbia* finally sighted the derelict, and after much difficulty got her in tow for Halifax. Ultimately, *Caldwell* reached Boston and the much-needed overhaul. *Roxborough*, caught south of Greenland in the same storm, was hit on 15 January 1943 by a giant sea that ripped bridge and wheelhouse completely open, killed the captain in his crushed cabin, and injured all hands in the pilothouse. Her surgeon, working 17 hours in an improvised operating room on the wildly pitching ship, managed to save all but one of the injured. After the storm, *Leamington* arrived in port with ice from two to ten feet thick on her bridge and forecastle. Such was the stability of the modified old flush deckers and the seamanship of their crews that they all survived this most grueling of tests.

On 11 April 1943, *Beverley*, crippled two days before in a collision that disabled her ASW gear, fell victim to a lurking U-boat. *St. Croix*, which had already sunk two Germans, was sunk by another in a running battle with a wolf pack on 20 September. Her survivors were taken aboard frigate HMS *Itchen* which was herself lost two days later. Only one man from *St. Croix* came home to Canada.

Age was beginning to tell on the material condition of the flush deckers. *Burnham's* engineering officer, inspecting her hull in dry dock in November 1942, found to his horror that rivets he tapped shucked out of her bottom plates in a shower of rust.

Though she had worked only six years of her life, the rust had been working all 23 years. Many of the old destroyers were obviously living on borrowed time. As new construction closed the gap between anti-submarine vessels needed and those on hand, most of the "Town" class were withdrawn to rear echelon duties, serving as training ships, tenders, aircraft practice targets, or depot and barracks ships. Many were laid up in reserve. Offers to return some of them to the U. S. Navy were politely declined. But departure from the front lines did not mean freedom from danger. *Rockingham* proved this by running over a mine and going down, 27 September 1944.

On the Canadian side, *Columbia*, while still engaged in active service, on 25 February 1944, found herself out of position in a heavy fog with her radar acting up. The next minute she ran head-on into a cliff in Motion Bay, Newfoundland. Since she never touched bottom, this unusual accident may not have been a grounding, but her bow was thoroughly smashed just the same. Inasmuch as she was already slated for retirement, it was decided to reduce her to a hulk for the storage of fuel and ammunition removed from ships refitting at Liverpool, Nova Scotia. *St. Clair* became a submarine depot ship at Halifax until August 1944, when, being declared unfit for further service, she was converted to a damage-control and fire-fighting hulk for training crews under the most realistic conditions. In this way the "unserviceable" old ship outserved many of her newer sisters.

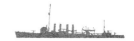

Last of the 50 to be lost was ex-*Churchill*, transferred to Russia in early 1944 in lieu of part of the surrendered Italian fleet. Renamed *Dyeyatelni* (Active), she was torpedoed and sunk while escorting a convoy in the White Sea, 16 January 1945. Several of the British ships that had been operating out of Canadian ports as local convoy escorts were considered so worn-out and unseaworthy that they were paid off and sold for scrap in Canada when the rest of their mates were retired from combat service. One final member of the "Town" class ended up far off the beaten track. *Lewes*, the most widely traveled of the 50, was the only one to see service in the Middle and Far Eastern theaters. Sent to South Africa in March 1943 to serve as an aircraft target and training ship, she moved on to Ceylon in 1944, then in January 1945, was sent to Sydney, Australia, where she finished out her career doing more of the same kind of duty.

Simplified Plan
of a
FLUSH – DECK
FOUR – STACK
DESTROYER

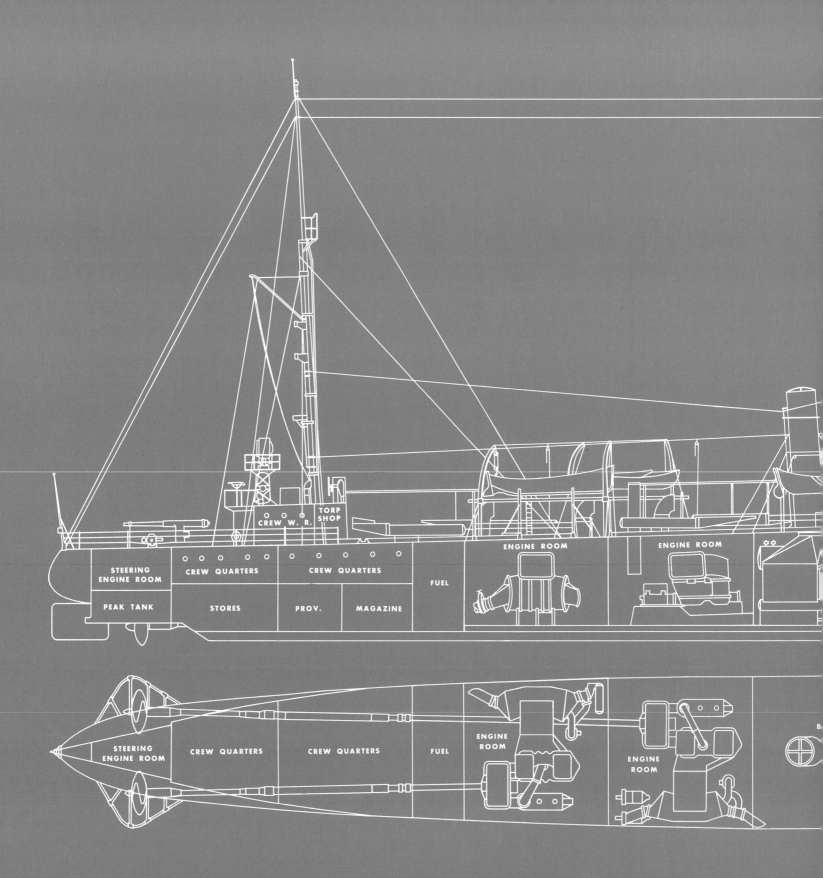

STEERING
ENGINE ROOM

CREW W. R.

TORP
SHOP

CREW QUARTERS

CREW QUARTERS

FUEL

ENGINE ROOM

ENGINE ROOM

PEAK TANK

STORES

PROV.

MAGAZINE

STEERING
ENGINE ROOM

CREW QUARTERS

CREW QUARTERS

FUEL

ENGINE
ROOM

ENGINE
ROOM

B

GALLEY

SEA CABIN

RADIO ROOM

CHART HOUSE

BOILER ROOM

ENG. OFF. CABIN

CAPTAIN'S CABIN

WARDROOM

CPO QUARTERS

CREW W. R.

STORES

LAMP ROOM

CREW QUARTERS

CREW QUARTERS

STORES

CHAIN LOCKER

PAINT LOCKER

PEAK TANK

FUEL

MAGAZINE

FUEL

FUEL

FUEL

SOUND ROOM

PEAK TANK

OFFICE

PANTRY

S. R.

S. R.

W.R.

BOILER ROOM

PASSAGE

WARDROOM

CPO QUARTERS

CREW W. R.

STORES

ENG. OFF. CABIN

CAPTAIN'S CABIN

S. R.

S. R.

W.R.

STORES

General Statistics

Standard Displacement...............1,090 tons
Length Over-all ....314′ 4″
Beam ....30′ 6″
Maximum Draft...........................12′
Main Battery ....4-4″/50
Antiaircraft Battery ....1-3″/23
Torpedo Battery ....12-21″ torpedo tubes
Antisubmarine Weaponry...not in original design
Boilers 4
Machinery ....2 geared turbines, 25,200 SHP
Designed Speed....................... 35 knots
Quarters Available ....9 officers, 144 men

These figures, from *Ships' Data U. S. Naval Vessels 1935*, are for the *Wickes* (DD-75). The statistics for any one ship might vary slightly from those for any other.

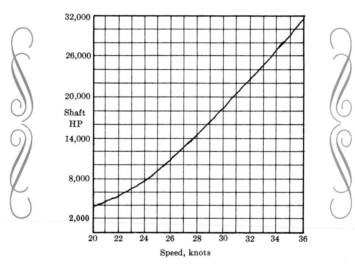

Horsepower vs Speed Curve *USS Hamilton* (DD-141) (Displacement 1,250 tons)

Data on *Hamilton* and other destroyers indicates the following variation in horsepower required to make 35 knots for different displacements:

1,163 tons—25,100 SHP
1,250 tons—29,300 SHP
1,305 tons—32,400 SHP

Data adapted from "Full Scale Trials on a Destroyer" by H. E. Saunders and A. S. Pitre in Society of Naval Architects and Marine Engineers *Transactions*, Vol. 41, 1933, pp. 243-295.

Back on the American side of the Atlantic also, things had been happening to the rest of the old flush deckers during the time their sisters were serving under European flags. When war between the great powers finally came, in September 1939, most of the newly recommissioned old-timers were sent out on Neutrality Patrol, as the fleet tried desperately to bring itself to fighting pitch, and the general public, isolated from the squabbling nations of Europe, still dreamed of peace. In the ferment of naval activity, realization of the true scope of the U-boat menace brought sonar back to the fore. Sound schools were established on the West Coast at San Diego and on the East Coast at New London in 1939. Because of the difficult operating conditions off the New England coast, the East Coast school was soon moved to Key West. Flush deckers were the first U. S. destroyers to carry echo-ranging sonar, and for training purposes, a division or so of them was stationed at each sound school.

President Roosevelt's Neutrality Zone did not remain neutral for long, as far as the ships patrolling it were concerned. It was while carrying mail to U. S. Marines in Iceland, on 4 September 1941, that the aging *Greer* (DD-145) got into a cat-and-mouse game with a German sub by tracking and reporting the *U-652* to a nearby British patrol plane. When the mouse let fly a salvo of torpedoes, the cat nimbly combed their wakes and proceeded to drop "ash cans" on the U-boat. It was the first attack made on a U. S. Navy ship in World War II, though back in April the new destroyer *Niblack* (DD-424) dropped depth charges on a suspected U-boat, also near Iceland. More were soon to come. The very next month *Reuben James* (DD-245), while escorting a British convoy west of Iceland, was hit by a Nazi torpedo and sank within minutes with over 100 of her crew. Thus, a flush decker was the first U. S. warship sunk in World War II—31 October 1941, over a month before the formal entry of the United States into the war. Shortly thereafter, another "first" was scored by *Leary* (DD-158) when she made the first known radar contact by a U. S. warship on an enemy submarine. This occurred on 19 November 1941.

By now, the youngest of the flush deckers was over 19 years old, a ripe old age for any destroyer. By every standard, the class was obsolete, and its members had chalked up a record that clearly entitled them to honorable retirement. But the tough-

est service was yet to come, and soon. *Ward* (DD-139), Mare Island's pride of World War I, under Lieutenant W. W. Outerbridge, was patrolling the entrance to Pearl Harbor early in the morning of 7 December 1941, when a suspicious object, soon identified as a small submarine, was sighted heading for the net gate. The craft was in a closed security zone where there could be no doubt as to its hostility. *Ward's* guns barked at the tiny conning tower, her depth charges blasted the midget hull to the bottom, and her radio crackled a warning to the fleet command. It was one more warning that failed to get through on that fateful day. Before the destroyer reached her berth, Japanese planes were strewing carnage on the moored battle force. Other flush deckers were in Pearl Harbor that morning, but the only two still classed as destroyers were *Schley* (DD-103), under overhaul and inoperative, and *Chew* (DD-106), which not only shot down a Japanese plane with her old 3-inch gun but depth-charged sound contacts as well. The rest had been converted to minelayers, minesweepers, and seaplane tenders. Nevertheless, those that could, sortied and fired at the attackers with all the weapons they could bring to bear. *Breese* dropped depth charges on what may have been a midget sub, possibly the one discovered by skin divers and raised in 1960. *Montgomery's* men shot an enemy aviator who refused to be taken prisoner from his sinking plane, but *Gamble*, encountering a surfacing submarine outside the harbor, found herself firing at USS *Thresher* before recognition signals could be exchanged. No harm was done.

Probably the worst ordeal of all was in store for the 13 flush deckers of DesRon 29 in the Asiatic Fleet. Under flagship *Paul Jones* (DD-230), these ships fought desperately as their area of operations was slowly strangled by the tentacles of the advancing Japanese fleet. Although their battle was primarily a surface-ship fight, *Edsall* (DD-219) assisted in sinking submarine *I-124* on 20 January 1942. In an effort to break the Japanese stranglehold, *John D. Ford* (DD-228) led *Pope* (DD-225), *Parrott* (DD-218), and *Paul Jones* in a surprise attack on invasion shipping at Balikpapan, Borneo, on 24 January. Slicing at 27 knots between the Japanese merchantmen, the four destroyers let fly with torpedoes and 4-inch shells. The surprise was complete: four transports and an escort were sunk. But the Japanese advance continued inexorably.

In confused fighting in and around the Java Sea under an improvised American-British-Dutch-Australian command (ABDAFloat), the old "cans" rapidly were lost or damaged, slipping away like the ten little Indians. On 15 February, *Bulmer* (DD-222) and *Barker* (DD-213) were so shaken up by six hours of intensive bombing from unopposed Nipponese aircraft that they had to be sent to Australia for repairs. *Peary* (DD-226), caught while under overhaul at Cavite, had almost been lost in the initial bombing on 10 December 1941. A bomb hit her superstructure and killed eight crewmen, and torpedo warheads started to erupt in the flaming overhaul shops on the wharf alongside. The valiant minesweeper *Whippoorwill*, after two failures, got a line aboard and pulled the helpless destroyer clear, whereupon *Pillsbury* (DD-227) came alongside and passed hoses across to put out the fire. Retiring toward Australia, *Peary* escaped further bomb and torpedo attacks (including one by the Royal Australian Air Force) and reached Darwin on New Year's Day. After escorting a troop reinforcement convoy to Portuguese Timor, she was back in Darwin harbor on 19 February when enemy bombers jumped the shipping there. Among other ships present was *William B. Preston* (AVD-7) tending a brood of Catalina seaplanes. The two flush deckers fought back desperately, but both were hit. *Peary*, zigzagging through the cluttered harbor, took five bombs in succession and went down in flames, her machine guns firing to the last. *William B. Preston* was one of the few ships to survive the Darwin holocaust.

Meanwhile, in the Java Sea things were getting worse. Dispersed in ports all over the Indonesian archipelago, the American destroyers were never again to operate together as a squadron. In an unsuccessful Dutch-American attack on the Japanese in the Badoeng Strait off Bali, on 20 February, *Stewart* (DD-224) took shell hits from enemy destroyers which smashed her steering machinery, forcing her to limp to dry dock in Soerabaja. The others became more and more decrepit and their stores of ordnance and supplies lower and lower until only four—*John D. Edwards* (DD-216), *Paul Jones*, *Alden* (DD-211), and *John D. Ford*—were fit to operate with the Allied fleet in its desperate last battle, that of the Java Sea, 27 February 1942. Ironically, the sole damage inflicted on the Japanese was from the 4-inch guns of the four pipers, oldest

ships in the Allied forces and the only ships of Dutch Admiral Doorman's 15 assorted cruisers and destroyers to survive the battle and subsequent small actions. Refueling at Soerabaja, they departed immediately for Australia, leaving only cripples behind to make their final desperate efforts to escape. Few got out of the trap. *Edsall*, damaged by the premature explosion of one of her own depth charges, and *Whipple* (DD-217), injured by collision with the Dutch cruiser *De Ruyter*, had continued to make themselves useful at Tjilatjap on the south coast of Java. After rescuing survivors from sunken *Langley* and *Pecos*, seaplane tender and oiler, respectively, the two destroyers retired independently on 1 March, but *Edsall* was trapped by a force of Japanese battleships and cruisers and went down under the point-blank fire of the cruiser *Ashigara*. Her five survivors died in prison camp, and it was not until 1952 that the fate of the old destroyer was established. On the same night, *Pillsbury* and *Parrott* slipped out of Tjilatjap in a raging storm with a nondescript group of slow gunboats and auxiliaries making the last dash for security. *Pillsbury* and gunboat *Asheville* went down with all hands, probably sunk by a squadron of enemy cruisers and destroyers. *Pope*, too, met her end on this date. She was attempting to flee Soerabaja with the British *Exeter* and *Encounter* by way of Sunda Strait, the passage between Java and Sumatra. The U. S. warship, worn-out and with Number 3 boiler out of commission, saw her consorts go down under Japanese gunfire, while only a providential rain squall kept her from immediate destruction. The respite was short-lived—aircraft soon found her again. Crippled by a near bomb hit, she was abandoned and sinking from demolition charges set off by her own crew when the pursuing Japanese cruisers appeared on the horizon and sent her to the bottom with a final 8-inch salvo. In all this melee only one man was lost, killed, ironically, by a demolition charge. All but 27 of the rest survived prison camps to be repatriated after the war. *Stewart*, left behind in dry dock, had been hopelessly trapped when shores gave way, dropping her over on her port side, in which state she took a bomb hit. On 2 March her crew set off demolition charges and sank the floating dry dock with *Stewart's* remains in it. The Asiatic Fleet was no more.

In the Pacific fighting for the rest of the war, destroyer action demanded a degree of gun power

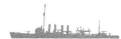

and endurance that was thought beyond the capabilities of the surviving flush deckers. Those that remained served in auxiliary roles, with the exception of a few on local guard duty, at sound school, and in the Aleutian theater. *Fox* (DD-234) thus spent most of the war operating between Seattle and Alaska, usually trying to find subs to attack, but on one occasion, in October 1942, escorting four Soviet submarines to San Francisco. *King* (DD-242) was another that saw duty in the Aleutians, on one occasion coming to grief on the beach off the Adak airfield, whence she was extricated only by the strenuous efforts of her crew and the Seabees.

The survivors of DesRon 29 made their way back to the East Coast where they joined their sisters already engaged in the Battle of the Atlantic, for anything that could carry a depth charge was needed to fight the U-boats. For sheer ruggedness, the struggle to bring men and materials across the stormy Atlantic in the face of the Nazi wolf packs could not be surpassed. Beginning months before Pearl Harbor the U. S. flush deckers already in the Atlantic pitched in with their sisters under the White Ensign, who had been fighting this battle since 1940. Altered for escort work, their stacks and masts were lowered, antiaircraft machine guns added, and torpedo tubes reduced by half. In many, the 4-inch guns were replaced by dual-purpose 3-inch/50s which could strike at aerial targets, and Number 4 stack and boiler were removed to give space for more fuel tanks and other improvements. Others were converted to auxiliary types or assigned to essential but unglamorous training and experimental duties.

The desperate months of 1942 when everything afloat was flung into the battle for the Atlantic—including ships in poor material condition and with green crews—saw the inevitable heavy casualties. *Truxtun* (DD-229), en route back from Reykjavik, Iceland, and cargo ship *Pollux* ran aground on the rugged Newfoundland coast in a heavy sleet storm, neither ship aware that the other was in trouble. At dawn on 18 February 1942, attempts were made to get ashore by line and life raft. Twenty-nine men from the *Truxtun* made it to safety and sent for help, but by 0830 the ship began to break apart and roll over, and the captain gave all hands permission to swim for it. Rescuers arriving at about this time waded deep into the surf to pull exhausted swimmers to safety, but the ship had broken into three pieces and man after man, including the captain, was swept off the wreckage to death in the frigid, oil-slicked seas. When a dory, hauled overland to the scene, finally reached the wreck, there were only three men left aboard. Of all her crew, just 41 were saved. *Pollux's* crew was able to reach the shore, but the ship herself did not long survive.

Jacob Jones (DD-130), named after an earlier destroyer sunk by a German sub in the First World War, was destined to share the fate of her namesake. Struck off Cape May in the early morning of 28 February, her bow and stern were blown off by three or four torpedo hits. Most of the crew died at once; many were killed in the water when the depth charges of the sinking ship blew up. There were only nine survivors. Accidents were common. *Semmes* (AG-24) rammed and sank HMS *Senateur Duhamel* off the North Carolina coast, 6 May 1942. In the Caribbean, *Blakeley* (DD-150) was some miles off the coast guarding immobilized French warships at Martinique when, on 25 May, a torpedo hit her bow and blew away all the ship forward of the bridge. Emergency repairs were made at Fort-de-France, Martinique; Port Castries, St. Lucia; and San Juan, Puerto Rico, where an anchor was improvised out of a truck axle, differential, and springs welded to a piece of railroad track, and she limped back to Philadelphia to have a new bow spliced on. *Sturtevant* (DD-240) came to an ignominious end when she blundered into a supposedly friendly minefield at Key West and was lost with three dead on 26 April. Then on 18 September, *Barney* (DD-149), while escorting a convoy from Trinidad to Guantanamo, rammed *Greer's* stern. The dislodged depth charges went off under *Barney's* keel. Both ships put into Willemstad, Curaçao, then crept home to Charleston for repairs. (After this *Greer* seems to have made a career of collisions, for on 15 October 1943 she rammed and sank USS *Moonstone* off the Atlantic coast, and on 30 November while seeking to avoid one tanker in Norfolk harbor was struck by another, the USS *Rapidan*.)

For the landings in North Africa, three of the flush deckers were practically written off as expendable and stripped down for desperate assault missions. *Cole* (DD-155) and *Bernadou* (DD-153), loaded with specially trained troops, were given the task of getting into Safi harbor and seizing port facilities before they could be sabotaged by the French defenders. Creeping in past the breakwater on 8 November 1942, the two ships were greeted

with point-blank fire from the French batteries, but came through unscathed. *Dallas* (DD-199), the third member of the team, had an even more hazardous assignment—after the defending forts surrendered she was to slip through the harbor of Mehedia, past nets and booms, and up the shallow and winding Sebou River to Port Lyautey, and land Army Rangers to seize the airfield. The time arrived but the stubborn French refused to surrender their forts on schedule. *Dallas* was ordered up the river, anyway, in broad daylight. Ramming through the boom and churning her way through mud banks while French gunners ashore fired 75mm. at her, she scraped bottom most of the way. At one point, she was making turns for 25 knots in order to crawl along at five, but she finally landed her Rangers eight miles up the river on 10 November. Missions accomplished, all three destroyers were awarded the Presidential Unit Citation for their work.

At about this same time, other flush deckers were struggling against wintry weather in the North Atlantic. *Overton* (DD-239), with two boilers inoperative, was sent to meet the speedy *Queen Elizabeth*, 500 miles at sea, and escort her to port. Running at her best speed in a full gale, she shifted fuel to the port tanks to counterbalance the force of the wind. Waves smashed the splinter shield of Number 1 gun, leaked through the forecastle deck, carried away the bridge windshield, caused a six-foot crack in the main deck at the engine room hatch, and washed two depth charges out of the racks, but the destroyer kept up the pace. When she finally hove to in the lee of the land, her unbalanced fuel tanks caused her to take an 11-degree list to port. But in the words of her skipper's official report, "Other than this superficial damage the ship had weathered the trip very well."

As the Battle of the Atlantic reached its climax, task groups built around escort carriers—hunter-killer groups—took an increasing part in the struggle against the undersea menace. In this vital and arduous service, flush deckers took an active role. Particularly successful were those working with the USS *Bogue* in Task Groups 21.12 and 21.13. In this service, the old destroyers *Lea* (DD-118) and *DuPont* (DD-152), and the *Greene* (AVD-13), *Belknap* (AVD-8), *Osmond Ingram* (AVD-9), *George E. Badger* (AVD-3), and *Clemson* (AVD-4)—although nominally seaplane tenders, the last five named were actually employed as destroyers at

the time and were reclassified as such a short time later—earned Presidential Unit Citations.

Credit for sinking German submarines was given to the following flush deckers, either singly or in company with other ships:

Roper—*U-85*, 14 April 1942—the first German submarine sunk by a U.S. ship in World War II.

George E. Badger—*U-613*, 23 July 1943.

Borie—*U-405*, 1 November 1943.

George E. Badger, Clemson, DuPont and *Osmond Ingram*—*U-172*, 13 December 1943.

Schenck—*U-645*, 24 December 1943.

Borie's encounter with *U-405* was to be her last. The U-boat, possibly damaged and unable to submerge, surfaced to shoot it out, but *Borie*, getting in position to ram, rode clear up on her adversary's deck. For ten minutes she hung there, both crews shooting wildly with anything they could get their hands on. Finally breaking apart, the injured submarine tried to creep away, pursued by the wounded destroyer, which managed to get the advantage with depth charges and a salvo of gunfire into the submarine's conning tower. The enemy called it quits and abandoned ship, but the victorious *Borie*, her forward engine room hull plates crushed, was in trouble too. Damage-control parties struggled all night and the next day to stem the flooding, but heavy seas gave them no respite. At last, on the evening of 2 November, when it appeared doubtful that she could be kept afloat through the night, her skipper ordered his men overside to the waiting *Barry* (DD-248) and *Goff* (DD-247). Even so the sea claimed the lives of 27 men in the raging waves. Next morning, the waterlogged hulk was sent to the bottom by bombs from the planes of *Borie's* own carrier.

On the day before Christmas of that winter, still another flush decker went down. *Leary* (DD-158) and *Schenck* (DD-159) had made radar contact on several disappearing targets, and *Schenck* bore in to sink *U-645* with well-placed depth charges. But while *Leary* was closing in on sonar, two torpedoes knocked out all of her power. Salvage was out of the question, and while all hands were going over the side, another torpedo hit and sent the ship quickly to the bottom. Her commanding officer, Commander James E. Kyes, last seen giving his life jacket to one of the steward's mates, and 96 others went down with the ship. *Lea* (DD-118) narrowly escaped sinking a few days later, 31 De-

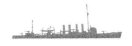

HMS Clare, *formerly USS Abel P. Upshur (DD-193), was rebuilt into an ocean escort in 1941, losing two boilers and two stacks in the process. The loss in speed, perhaps eight knots, was made up for by a gain in range. There is an open bridge atop the pilot house.*

HMS Lewes, *formerly USS Conway (DD-70), another ocean escort, is at center left as she appeared in 1942. Her weaponry consisted entirely of antiaircraft guns, depth charges in racks, and K guns.*

HMS Leeds, *formerly USS Conner (DD-72), is at center right as she appeared in August 1942. Just as the Lewes, her half sister, she carried US-made 3-inch guns and single 40-mm. weapons. She was built with the three stacks seen here. For her original appearance, see the Stockton (DD-73) on page 4.*

HMCS St. Francis, *formerly USS Bancroft (DD-256), near the end of the war, when she was tender to the net training station at Annapolis Basin, Nova Scotia. In 1945, while under tow to an American scrap yard, she collided with a merchant ship and sank.*

cember 1943, when she was rammed by the SS *Elihu Yale*. Her after engine room was flooded and salt water contaminated all of her boilers. Helpless, she spent New Year's Eve wallowing in mid-Atlantic until picked up and towed to Boston by the seagoing tug USS *Cherokee*.

The last flush decker to be lost on the Atlantic side was *Parrott* (DD-218). This ship had escaped from everything the Japanese had to offer in the Java Sea, only to be sunk in Norfolk harbor on 2 May 1944. While backing out of her berth she was rammed by the SS *John Morton*, and three men were killed. She was beached and later salvaged, but considered not worth repairing.

Other less violent adventures were experienced by the flush deckers in the course of their wanderings about the Atlantic and Mediterranean. *Noa* took time out from fighting, in August 1942, to deliver 21 million Cuban pesos to the treasury in Havana. *MacLeish* (DD-221), at one time assigned to escort the *Queen Mary*, had to give up when her best speed of 25 knots proved too slow for the *Queen*. Assigned to humbler duties thereafter, she escorted one of the weirdest convoys in history to Cherbourg shortly after the Normandy landings. This unusual group consisted of self-propelled oil lighters, Army harbor tugs towing railroad barges and floating cranes, and similar harbor craft. On this trip, *MacLeish* had no difficulty keeping up. At that date, most of the flush deckers had been withdrawn from front-line service, so none of them took part in the invasion of Northern France, although several were active in the Mediterranean during the Southern landings. As if she were not content with all the "firsts" the class had chalked up early in the war, *Semmes*, the New London sound school ship, joined in the last submarine killing on 6 May 1945. Using her special sonar gear to pinpoint the bottomed submarine, she helped deliver the coup de grace to *U-853* off Block Island.

Picking up the careers of the flush deckers that had been converted to other types, we find that the eight DMs put in an action-packed tour during which they covered the Pacific. The early months were spent laying defensive minefields throughout the South Pacific, and performing other chores, such as landing parties of Marines on deserted little islands in mid-ocean. *Gamble*, off Guadalcanal, lived up to her destroyer training by sinking the Japanese

submarine *I-123* on 29 August 1942. Other DMs made the run to Alaska to lay their protective minefields in that area. *Sicard* on such duty on 10 May 1943 plowed into the eight-year-old destroyer *Macdonough*. Despite a badly crumpled bow, she then proceeded to redress the injury by towing the crippled destroyer to Adak. That same month, *Preble* in the South Pacific carried out an unusual rescue operation when she salvaged four motor torpedo boats. They had been deck-loaded on a merchantman and had floated free when she was torpedoed and sunk. On the offensive side, *Gamble*, *Breese*, and *Preble* pulled off a real coup by sneaking a minefield across Blackett Strait in which the Japanese destroyers of the "Tokyo Express" became ensnared a few days later. On 8 May, *Kurashio* was sunk, and *Oyashio* and *Kagero* crippled, to be polished off next day by U. S. aircraft. Three months earlier, on 1 February, destroyer *Makigumo* was similarly sunk in a field laid by the DMs off Guadalcanal. Such operations were not without their hazards for the minelayers, for, on 25 August 1943, *Montgomery* knifed into *Preble*, peeling off 20 feet of bow. Both were repaired. Thirteen months later, during the Peleliu landings, *Preble* was assigned to destroy a suspected field of acoustic mines by steaming along the edge of the supposed field, dropping depth charges every 200 yards and howling away on a special siren installed for this quixotic purpose. It was a shame that no explosions occurred to signal success in this bizarre operation!

The DMs couldn't get away with this sort of thing forever, and when the end came for *Montgomery* it was not as dramatic as might have been expected. Anchored in Ngulu Lagoon, near Palau, 17 October 1944, her lookouts spotted a Japanese mine drifting close aboard. While frantic efforts were being made to get under way, the ship swung down on the mine and touched it off. The resulting explosion blew a hole in the ship's side and flooded all of the engineering spaces. She was towed to Ulithi and repaired enough to get back to San Francisco under her own power, but there she was surveyed and decommissioned as beyond economical repair. By this stage of the war the old DMs had for the most part been relegated to secondary duties, but when the need arose *Gamble* was pressed into service to screen battleship *Nevada* in the bombardment line at Iwo Jima. Here, on 18 February 1945, she was suddenly jumped by a

With just over two months yet to live, the Reuben James (DD-245) passes through the Cape Cod Canal on 21 August 1941. She wears an unusual three-tone paint job. Hull number is beneath the bridge, World War I style. She was sunk off Iceland on 31 October 1941 while escorting a British convoy. Photo, courtesy Paul W. Hatch.

The Roper (DD-147) was the first U.S. ship to sink a U-boat in World War II when she destroyed the U-85, 14 April 1942, off the Virginia coast. Just as did most of her sisters at this time, she mounted six 3-inch, dual-purpose guns, six torpedo tubes, two depth charge racks, K guns, and a few 20-mm.

Japanese plane which put two bombs into her engine rooms. Though flooding was controlled and the crippled ship towed back to Saipan, she was too far gone for repairs and was scuttled outside the harbor, 16 July. By war's end, all but two of the flush-deck DMs had been downgraded to the AG (miscellaneous auxiliary) list, and only *Breese* and *Tracy* were retired as minelayers. *Tracy*, unlike most of her flush-deck sisters, stayed in the Pacific after the Japanese surrender, but her duty was, for a minelayer, ignominious. She became a minesweeper in all but official designation, and swept the Japanese coast until late October, during which period she was the first U.S. warship to enter Nagasaki harbor after the war.

The tide of alteration and conversion had been rolling on in other ways for some years, engulfing most of the remaining flush deckers in its flood. The use of these ships as high-speed minesweepers, already alluded to, was the result of experimentation going back a number of years. The concept was quite thoroughly tried out in *Manley* in 1935, but because the arrangements were not entirely satisfactory the gear was modified and transferred to *Gamble* where its use was perfected. In 1940 the full-time use of destroyers as fast minesweepers was formalized with the conversion and reclassification of *Dorsey* (DD-117) to DMS-1, closely followed by 17 of her sisters. Considerable structural change was made to the ships besides the addition of sweep gear, including the now familiar removal of a boiler and stack, elimination of all torpedo tubes, rearmament with 3-inch guns, and many internal improvements. To make room for the sweep gear aft, a false stern with a relatively broad deck was built over the narrow existing structure.

War found the fast minesweepers divided between the two coasts. Those in the Atlantic—*Palmer, Hogan, Howard, Stansbury,* and *Hamilton*—served primarily as ASW escorts, but did some minesweeping off Fedhala and Casablanca during the North African invasion. After another year of convoy runs they were deployed to the Pacific in December 1943, joining their sister "scrubwomen of the sea."

The Pacific 'sweeps had been seeing arduous service all this time, some in the Aleutians and others in the South Pacific. Alaskan duty was rough for the DMSs acting as convoy escorts. *Lamberton* recorded a 57-degree roll on one occasion, while *Wasmuth* became the victim of her own

depth charges. While escorting a convoy, including tanker *Ramapo*, in a raging gale, two of her "ash cans" were wrenched off by the waves and exploded close aboard, fatally wounding the ship. Despite the towering seas, the entire complement was transferred to *Ramapo* in a three-and-one-half-hour rescue, and the abandoned flush decker went to the deeps, 27 December 1942.

In the southern theater, the old DMSs were in on all the hectic operations connected with the Solomons landings, sweeping the beach approaches and engaging in general support operations. *Long* got in her ASW licks by helping to down *I-23* on 29 January 1942. After the battle of Savo Island, *Hopkins* doubled as a tug and attempted to tow the crippled heavy cruiser *Astoria* to safety. The cruiser needed 220-volt electricity, but the old *Hopkins* could only supply 110. No matter; she was soon sent away to develop a submarine contact, and *Astoria* sank soon after. On 10 November 1942, *Southard* got herself a Japanese submarine—*I-172*—with depth charges and 4-inch gunfire. *Hovey* had an unusual experience in October of that year when she encountered the USS *Vireo*, abandoned and adrift south of Guadalcanal. It seems that the former minesweeper, then a fleet tug with a top speed of only ten knots, was in company with the destroyer *Meredith* (DD-434) when a superior enemy task force was reported just over the horizon. Taking the crew of the tug aboard, the destroyer hightailed it for home but was sunk anyway, while the *Vireo* was completely overlooked. After drifting several days before being found, she was taken in tow by *Hovey*, which later furnished a temporary crew and brought the derelict back to New Caledonia.

Zane and *Trever* had a narrow escape when a superior Japanese force caught them near Tulagi on 25 October. Despite the best the DMSs' old engines could put out, the enemy soon closed to 13,000 yards and were bracketing the fleeing pair with hits and near misses when some American dive bombers providentially appeared and turned the pursuers' attention skyward. The next June, off New Georgia, *Zane* had another close call. Aground on a reef, she was attacked by a flight of aircraft, just as the tug USS *Rail* was pulling her off, but *Zane* fought off the planes while she was still under tow, and managed to get away.

Through the rest of 1942 and 1943 the DMSs conducted escort, fire support, survey, and rescue

With her mast removed to cut down the chance of her being seen, the Bernadou (DD-153) steams east across the Atlantic, en route to an assault landing at Safi, French North Africa, on the night of 8 November 1942. Fourth funnel and boiler have been replaced by fuel tanks to increase her range.

The John D. Ford, one of eight destroyers to survive the destruction of the old Asiatic Fleet at the hands of the Japanese Navy, as she appeared at Mare Island, California, in August 1942, five months after the end of the Java Sea campaign. She has received an air search radar, K guns, and half a dozen 20-mm. guns in place of her mainmast, midships searchlight platform, and half of her torpedo battery. Her after 4-inch gun now has a splinter shield.

missions, in addition to their minesweeping duties. In September 1944, *Hovey, Southard, Perry, Long,* and *Hamilton* teamed up, with DM *Montgomery* as mine-destruction ship, for the Palau invasion. On 13 September, while sweeping at 14 knots, *Perry,* which was following *Southard* in supposedly safe, swept water, was lifted several feet by a mine exploding under her bow. Listing sharply to port, she started to settle and crewmen began to go over the side. *Preble,* which, as we have seen, came to Palau to destroy acoustic mines with depth charges and a siren, attempted to come alongside, but the men and a whaleboat in the water got in the way. Then, as she tried to nose in alongside her stricken sister, lookouts spotted a mine about two fathoms under the surface between the two ships. By some ticklish maneuvering, *Preble* extricated herself and made an approach from a different angle, but by this time *Perry* had swung around with her bow close to shore and all but a handful of her crew had abandoned ship. Still, *Preble* managed to get a hawser across and, backing through mines dimly visible beneath the surface, started to haul the cripple out, stern first. At this point the towline parted. Undaunted, *Preble* made still another try, this time sending a boarding party over. With the ship's forecastle awash and snipers firing small arms from the nearby shore, the party went about the destruction of radar and other classified material. They were still aboard when she rolled over, and they calmly clambered onto her upturned keel and back into their boat as the *Perry* went down.

More amphibious operations culminated in January 1945 with a big sweep into Lingayen Gulf, led by the DMSs. During the approaches the little ships were shadowed ominously by Japanese airplanes, which attacked the flotilla relentlessly, but without success, until the morning of 6 January. The ships had just made their first sweep for mines across the bay approaches when suicide planes suddenly plummeted into *Long* and APD *Brooks,* which had an Underwater Demolition Team aboard to help clear the beach. *Long,* hit on the port side directly under the bridge, was soon wreathed in flames and explosions. No sooner had her survivors abandoned ship and boarded *Hovey* when a second plane, smashing into the same area as the first, broke the vessel's back and she capsized and sank. That same evening, *Southard* took a kamikaze aboard which cut her main steam lines and left her dead in the

water. Her crew labored all night making repairs, and morning found her back on the job. At 0500 on 7 January, *Hovey* took a plane and a torpedo almost simultaneously in her starboard beam and went down in minutes with 22 of her own crew plus 24 from sunken *Long* and crippled *Brooks. Chandler* moved in to pick up survivors. That afternoon, *Palmer,* hit by two bombs from a near-miss suicide plane, also took the final plunge with 28 of her crew.

Others of the class had not been inactive during this period. *Chandler* got credit for an "assist" in killing *I-185,* on 22 June 1944, while *Trever* was one of the fleet that got mixed up with the typhoon of 18 December 1944. Passing directly into the eye of the storm, she was buffeted by 90-knot winds and mountainous waves that carried away much topside gear. A man washed overboard was miraculously recovered, after a two-hour search; his only injury was a badly broken leg. Newer and stronger ships fared worse than the veteran *Trever* in this storm, but her damage was sufficient to bring her fighting days to a close.

After Lingayen decimated the DMS ranks, many of those remaining were sent back to the States, designated AG and relegated to menial support tasks, in which they joined *Boggs* and *Lamberton,* who had spent most of the war in target-towing duties not unlike their old mobile target days. *Lamberton,* known as "Target-Towing Tessie," never fired a shot at an enemy target. Instead she was frequently on the receiving end of some wild salvos from supposedly friendly cruisers and destroyers. *Elliot,* also detailed to target-towing, was distinguished mainly by having Lieutenant Commander Thruston B. Morton, later a U. S. Senator from Kentucky, assigned as her skipper.

When the rest were sent back stateside, *Dorsey, Hopkins,* and *Southard* stayed on at Okinawa with MinRon 20. At war's end, they were engaged in the biggest sweep operation ever undertaken, covering 7,200 square miles in the East China Sea. After some 600 U. S. and Japanese mines had been swept, the operation was called off as a result of the peace negotiations. *Hopkins* participated in the Tokyo Bay sweeps on 30 August, then rejoined her sisters at Okinawa, where they were preparing to return to the States. In a typhoon on 12 September her starboard quarter was ripped open by a drifting barge. *Southard* had been so badly damaged by previous pounding against a camel in heavy swells that she

By November 1942 the Alden, another Asiatic Fleet veteran, had her funnels cut down and reduced to three in number, and all her hull ports plated over. The blast shield on the face of the bridge had gone, but the big windows remained. The barrage balloons in the background are guarding Mare Island Navy Yard.

The Semmes (AG-24) on experimental duty, photographed before the war (center right) by Lieutenant Commander R. E. Bassler; and at the close of the war (center left). Notice her raked HF/DF antenna, aft, and the curious shape of her funnels in 1945.

The Lea (DD-118) in April 1943. She differs from the Alden, above, mainly in mounting six 3-inch guns rather than her original four 4-inch. The 3-inch could be used against aircraft; the 4-inch could not. Hedgehog is visible just forward of Lea's bridge, and an HF/DF antenna is at the truck. The hull number is beneath the group of men on the forecastle.

was already scheduled for survey, but the typhoon tore loose an antisubmarine net which fouled her screws. With no means of propulsion, she dragged anchor and grounded on a pinnacle where she hung until a tug pulled her free. *Dorsey*, the only one of the trio in reasonably good condition, was crowded with 69 passengers for the trip home. In this situation the worn-out ships were struck by still another typhoon on 9 October. This storm, the worst recorded in 20 years, with winds up to 125 knots, threw *Southard* up on a reef. *Dorsey*, dragging anchor, attempted to slip her cable but found it jammed with 118 fathoms out. Hampered by the drag of this weight, she was unable to maneuver and went aground with the waves breaking over her sides and lower spaces flooded. When things calmed down next day, her crew sadly hoisted their 180-foot homeward bound pennant on the wreck and abandoned ship. The two old ships were decommissioned and left where they lay. *Hopkins*, despite her injuries, survived and headed for home and the scrapyard, the last flush-deck DMS left to be stricken from the Navy List. The little DMSs, for all their humble target-towing, contributed so much to the war in the Pacific that they made off with no fewer than seven Navy Unit Commendations for their services.

The war service of the next group, the AVD seaplane tenders, could hardly have been more varied. Since each ship was equipped to support a squadron of Catalina flying boats, the nature of their work insured that they would be spread all over the oceans on more or less isolated stations. Those in the Atlantic ranged from Panama to the coasts of Greenland. While such lucky ones as *Clemson*, *Greene*, and *Osmond Ingram* enjoyed the tropical climes of the Caribbean and Panama, *George E. Badger* and *Goldsborough* shivered at Argentia. But the crew of *Belknap* thought they had the worst deal of all. En route to her station off Iceland, she was in trouble even before the shooting war started. Trying to get through a submarine-infested area, she was planing like a surfboard at 22 knots in a heavy following sea when she was pooped by a huge wave that jimmied up her stern and threw her port shaft out of line. Expecting an early return to the States, she got a quick and dirty repair job from the repair ship *Vulcan* at Hvalfjordur. Next she was ordered to send 15 men from her short-handed crew ashore every day to build a camp in the

freezing mud and howling wind. But when orders to return home arrived, they were addressed to sister ship *Goldsborough*. The winter of 1941-42 was misery. Heavy seas and 133-mile-an-hour winds sank five planes and three ship's boats and put an end to air operations, but couldn't quite put an end to *Belknap*. Dragging anchor and using her engines to maneuver, she managed to keep from being blown ashore. With the planes out of operation, morale on the tender sank lower and lower, not aided by a mere four hours of daylight when the sun shone at all. Finally, after nine months of this she was sent back to Charleston for overhaul. Stopping at Newport en route, her damaged propeller fell off at the first backing bell!

By 1943 the need for AVDs in the Atlantic had diminished, and the flush deckers were pressed into ASW service, then redesignated back to destroyers in December 1943 before being switched once again to transports. In the Pacific, things were slightly different, but not much. *Childs* and *William B. Preston* started the war in the Asiatic Fleet. *Childs* dodged the bombs in Manila Bay on 10 December 1941, air attacks at Menado, Celebes, and pursuing warships which almost trapped her at Kendari harbor. To escape the ubiquitous Japanese planes, she moved down to Exmouth Gulf, Australia, where she operated until ordered home in August 1944. *Preston's* experiences at Darwin have already been related. At the other end of the Pacific, AVDs operating in the Aleutians shared the miseries of their sisters in Iceland. *Hulbert* tended her brood at Amchitka, mothering a motor torpedo boat squadron as well for two weeks. But on 30 June 1943 she dragged anchor and went on the beach at Massacre Bay, Attu, washing up until she was high and dry on the sand. Twenty-one days of strenuous work by her crew and some nearby SeaBees finally got her afloat again, but it was back to San Diego and routine plane guard duties for her after that.

Williamson was another Alaska veteran with a record of adventure. In May 1942, just before the Japanese occupation of Kiska, she was called upon to rescue General Simon Bolivar Buckner when bad weather grounded his plane and left him stranded on that island during a reconnaissance visit. After the Japanese invasion, *Williamson* established an advanced base from which her PBYs bombed the occupying forces. While trying to pick up one of her planes in extremely rough seas on 26 June

Four just-converted destroyer minesweepers at Pearl Harbor in January 1941, still wearing light paint and big numbers. Both Perry (DMS-17) and Wasmuth (DMS-15) were to be lost during the war. Multi-colored design on the bow was the pre-war Mine Force emblem. Mainmast and torpedo tubes were removed, sweep gear added amidships and aft.

The Chandler (DMS-9) racing out of Pearl Harbor on 7 December 1941, looking for Japanese submarines. Two-tone paint, with light upper works, was standard in the Pacific Fleet at that time, along with small hull numbers on the bow.

The Hopkins (DMS-13) in September 1943, her decks cluttered with unstowed gear and stores. A broad false stern, reminiscent of the stern on the first six flush deckers, made room for the sweep gear.

1942. a wing clipped the depth charge rack on her stern and knocked two "ash cans" into the water. (The frequency with which this type of accident seems to have occurred is an indication of the touchiness of depth charges and the dangers involved in carrying them.) The resulting blast put one screw out of action and flooded several compartments. forcing her to limp back to Seattle for a refit. As the need for the old seaplane tenders lessened, *Williamson* was redesignated a DD and, as such, participated in the recapture of Attu in April and May of 1943. Then she was off to the South Pacific on ASW and escort duty. In April 1944. at Purvis Bay, she was given an unofficial conversion back to a seaplane tender, being modified to conduct under-way fueling of float observation planes attached to the amphibious assault forces. Trials were successful; and *Williamson* served in this capacity at Saipan. Guam, Iwo Jima, and Okinawa. thus finally bringing to fruition the line of development that had been tried and found wanting with *Charles Ausburn* in 1923 and *Noa* in 1939.

In the Guadalcanal area, *McFarland's* duties involved delivering emergency fuel supplies to the Marines at Henderson Field. Since the enemy controlled the air by day. this mission had to be carried out stealthily by night. While thus engaged on 16 October 1942. she was surprised by a flight of Japanese planes. After all but one had been shot down or driven off by friendly fighters, the last plane dropped its last bomb right on *McFarland's* depth charge racks, peeling off her whole stern topside but miraculously leaving propellers and shafts intact. Without a rudder, her skipper maneuvered her across the bay to Tulagi, where her crew camouflaged her with tropical foliage while they rigged a jury rudder of logs and an old steel plate. This got her to Noumea, where another makeshift was put on. Unfortunately, this one jammed hard over en route to Pearl Harbor, and the ship finally sidled into port dragging 40 fathoms of anchor chain from the starboard side to balance the pull of the jammed rudder. For their heroic action in saving the ship, her crew received the Presidential Unit Citation.

Ballard, too, played a valiant part in the Guadalcanal fighting. At one point she served Lieutenant Colonel Lewis Puller and his men in a dramatic fashion. The Marines, two companies strong, had been demonstrating against the Japanese up the Matanikau River when it was decided to send them around the seaward flank to Point Cruz. Here they were landed in what was thought—mistakenly—to be U. S.-held territory. Superior Japanese forces. cutting them off on a small hill inland from the beach, soon proved what the real situation was. Inside their defensive perimeter the harassed Marines took off their undershirts and spelled out the word "HELP" on the ground. But "Chesty" Puller was already on the way. Sensing trouble. he had boarded the *Ballard*, which obligingly brought him to the right place, where the trapped men semaphored their predicament to the little ship. Under a protective barrage from her deck guns. they fought their way back to the beach and were re-embarked in five Higgins boats under the command of Douglas A. Munro, a Coast Guard signalman who earned on that occasion his service's lone Medal of Honor for World War II—alas, an award that had to be made posthumously.

Despite arduous service, only one AVD was lost. *Thornton*, having done tours at Pearl Harbor, in the Aleutians, and in the South Pacific, was en route from Ulithi to Okinawa on 5 April 1945, when the oiler *Ashtabula* rammed her amidships moments after *Thornton* had sideswiped another AO, the *Escalante*. Towed to Kerama Retto. she was declared a total loss and beached in the graveyard of kamikaze victims there. Eventually all but four of the Pacific AVDs reverted back to destroyer classification and ended the war performing plane guard duties. Only *Childs*, *William B. Preston*, *Ballard*, and *Gillis* held the AVD designator at the war's end. even though they too ended their days as plane guards, for CVEs out of San Diego, after handing their seaplane-handling duties on to ships of the newer AVP classes.

In the most extensive conversion program of all, the amphibious forces acquired 32 flush deckers through the introduction of the high-speed transport (APD) class in 1940. This program originated with the much-altered *Manley*, when in 1938-39 she was reclassified AG-28 and given a hasty partial conversion to a shallow-draft troop transport to permit the accommodation of 120 Marines. So successful was this concept that she was back in the New York Navy Yard in the fall of 1939 for a full conversion. With the removal of the two forward stacks, both boilers from Number 1 fire room, all torpedo tubes and some of her guns (with the forward stacks

The **Preble (DM-20)** *in November 1943. In May 1943 she, in company with the* **Gamble (DM-15)** *and* **Breese (DM-18),** *laid 250 mines in Blackett Strait in the Central Solomons, resulting in the destruction of three Japanese destroyers. By the war's end Preble's aftermost 3-inch gun had been replaced by a 40-mm.*

Center left, the bow of the **Greer (DD-145).** *Center, the* **Childs (AVD-1)** *at the end of the war when she was plane guarding for escort carriers undergoing training on the West Coast. By 1945 many flush deckers had conical funnel tops. Center right, the stern of the Preble, showing centerline depth charge rack flanked by mine tracks.*

The **Williamson (AVD-2)** *in February 1942. One depth charge rack, two 3-inch guns, and a few 20-mm. constitute her armament.*

removed, one gun on the amidships deckhouse had nearly the same field of fire as the two original guns had), she was fitted to berth and support 200 Marines for a 48-hour period. As an indication of the type of amphibious operation envisioned at that early date, she was required to carry four machine guns on carts, one 75 mm. pack howitzer, ten boat guns, and ammunition for all of these—a total of 66,000 pounds of men and equipment. The Chief of Naval Operations pulled out all the stops to get this work completed in time for Fleet Landing Exercise Number 6 in January 1940, and shortly thereafter established the APD as an official ship type. *Manley*, of course, had the honor of becoming the first and name ship of the class.

Of the first six APDs (five were converted in the 1940 program), three were stationed on each coast when war erupted. During the early months, while the Navy was still licking its wounds, they engaged in amphibious exercises and patrol work. With the preparations for the Solomons campaign, all were concentrated in that sector. As originally envisioned, their mission was to land assault troops at invasion beachheads, and at this they excelled in the rough-and-tumble fighting among the South Pacific islands. Their small commando-type units were ideal for storming ashore at small ports like Tulagi, for making hit-and-run raids, or for mopping up isolated enemy detachments on small islands. Organized in Transport Division 12 and painted with splotchy jungle-green camouflage, they were known as the "green dragons." *McKean's* men became particularly attached to their party of Marine Raiders on Tulagi. On every return trip they brought in candy and cigarettes, sent pots of hot coffee ashore, and checked anxiously to see what casualties had been suffered in their absence.

With no tender to take care of them, the APDs had to take care of themselves as well as their Marines. Going around from unit to unit bumming supplies, their motley crews were tough-looking indeed. In the desperate fighting of those early months these poorly-armed auxiliary types found they were expected to act like the destroyers they once were in the face of the Japanese first team. This was asking too much, as was demonstrated by the loss of three of them in quick succession. *Colhoun*, having rushed a load of stores to the Marines entrenched on Guadalcanal on 30 August 1942, headed for sea to take an assigned ASW station.

Air raid warnings were soon received, followed by attacks from a flight of horizontal bombers that came in out of the sun at 10,000 feet. A hit, unusual in high-level horizontal bombing attacks, blew up her landing boats and guns, brought down the foremast, and set fires throughout the ship. The crew abandoned ship and all but 51 were picked up by tank lighters from ashore. An hour after midnight on 5 September, *Gregory* and *Little* were zigzagging off Lunga Point to avoid possible submarine attack, unable to retire to their accustomed berth at Tulagi because of poor visibility, when radar picked up a group of ships approaching rapidly. As the little APDs tried to make themselves inconspicuous, flares from a Catalina trying to be helpful and unaware that there were any U. S. ships around, illuminated them from behind. Despite answering shots from their 4-inch guns, the old flush deckers were quickly smothered under the gunfire of three Japanese destroyers coming up rapidly from astern. After only three minutes of this, *Gregory's* crew was ordered to abandon ship, while *Little* attempted to beach but lost steering control and was soon ablaze fore and aft. The survivors from both ships were machine-gunned by the onrushing enemy as they charged through at 25 knots. More than half of the crews were lost in the sinking and in the water, where some of them had to swim for 23 hours before reaching shore.

Manley, *Stringham*, and *McKean*, who came from the Atlantic to join their sisters, also saw plenty of action. Typical of their work, they once put Marine Raiders ashore to hit a Japanese-held village on Guadalcanal. Blowing up all the stores and equipment they could find, the Raiders used their Higgins boats to pull the Japanese field artillery into deep water, then re-embarked as quickly as they had come. On another occasion, *Manley* left Noumea carrying six torpedoes, towing two PT boats and escorting a merchant ship. She picked up a company of Raiders at Espiritu Santo and put them ashore at Lunga Point, then delivered the torpedoes and PT boats to Tulagi. Sometimes the APDs carried well over 200 Marines, soldiers, or members of Allied forces. Other missions consisted of putting a few guerrillas ashore, or picking up a handful of survivors from some isolated beach. Such work was dangerous, and *Stringham*, on 26 February 1943, hung herself up on a reef in the Russell

First of the flush deckers to be commissioned, the Manley (DD-74), which hoisted her pennant on 15 October 1917, is seen in 1939 as AG-28. In this rig, with boat davits in place of her torpedo tubes, she proved the high-speed, shallow-draft transport concept. Photo by courtesy of Ted Stone.

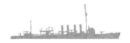

After further alterations in 1939-1940, the Manley became APD-1. This view shows her off the East Coast in 1941 or 1942 with four 36-foot Higgins landing craft in her davits, and berthing spaces for 200 Marines in place of two boilers. One 4-inch gun on the center line amidships replaces the two wing mounts. Four 20-mm. guns provide antiaircraft protection, and depth charges are much in evidence.

Islands. The combined efforts of her own and *Humphrey's* boats finally got her off, but it was back to Mare Island for repairs.

During late 1942 and early 1943, twelve more flush-deck DDs were released from patrol and escort duty on the West Coast and converted to APDs to replace those lost and to provide more of the same. Except for *Kane*, these rapidly joined the SoPac forces. *Kane*, purported by some to have been the real-life original for the ship in the novel "The Caine Mutiny," was ordered back to her old haunts in the fog-swept Aleutians, where she put 400 soldiers ashore on Attu on 11 May 1943. She followed this with clean-up landings on Agattu, Kiska, and other islands, before joining her sisters in the tropics. Of the four original members of TransDiv 12, *McKean* was now the only one left, but her time was up, too. Off Bougainville, on 17 November 1943, she took an air-launched torpedo in her after engine room. The entire after half of the ship was soon in flames, and wreckage jamming the whistle cord created a din which added to the confusion. A number of troops who abandoned ship were swept into the flaming oil from her ruptured tanks and were burned or drowned. As the ship finally slowed down and life rafts were launched, the forward magazine blew up, and *McKean* went to the bottom.

During this time, other flush deckers that had distinguished themselves in the antisubmarine war in the Atlantic were converted to APDs. The newcomers pitched right in with the veterans. *Overton*, teamed up with *Manley* for the Kwajalein invasion, was scheduled to put her troops ashore on Nenni islet, but in the darkness and the poor visibility from their rubber boats, the soldiers got themselves onto neighboring Gehh. Realizing their error, they crossed to the proper island, but returned next day to mop up some stranded Japanese seamen they had noticed on Gehh. This fortuitous conquest resulted in the capture of some 75 secret harbor charts from a ship beached on the island, a bit of booty that was a big help in future operations. Another of the new arrivals, *Dickerson*, was detained at Pearl Harbor for some experiments that were to revolutionize invasion tactics. Taking on board members of Underwater Demolition Team Number 3, she proceeded to Guam where her party reconnoitered and cleared the beaches selected for invasion. This early operation was so successful that it served as a model for trainees back in Hawaii.

Another of the UDT carriers, *Dent*, ran aground on an uncharted shoal, 22 December 1943. Patched up in Australia, she returned to join the operations at Guam but was found to be unseaworthy and sent back to the States for limited duty. *Gilmer* distinguished herself in the new UDT tactics, and also won the only surface engagement of the Marianas campaign when she shot up four Japanese coastal transports on 16 June 1944. Although she received over 20 shell hits in return, no serious casualties were suffered. A month later she teamed up with a DE to destroy a submarine, thus completing a record for versatility that it would be hard to beat.

A ship that tried was *Tattnall*. After being converted at Charleston in late 1943, she (with *Roper*, *Barry*, *Osmond Ingram*, and *Greene*) was detailed to the Mediterranean where the APDs landed Free French and U. S. commandos on islands off the southern coast of France, and later put Senegalese garrison troops ashore. As a sample of her activities during the invasion, she transported wounded, picked up survivors from a sunken German ship, transferred prisoners of war, supplied stores and water to troops ashore, salvaged 73 rubber boats, delivered guard mail, performed ASW patrol and escort duties, and sent her boats to salvage the grounded *PT-556* from under the noses of hostile shore batteries. After ticking off these chores, her commanding officer suggested that the APD classification really stood for "all-purpose destroyer"! Following the landings in southern France, all of the European APDs headed for the Panama Canal and the Pacific theater. Among them were six former AVDs that had reverted to DDs, and were now entering the third stage of their metamorphosis.

Other APDs were setting records in practically every landing operation in the Pacific. Despite the new UDT operations, old-fashioned landings were still needed in many areas. *Sands* put ashore what is believed to have been the first U. S. landing party on Ulithi, where she picked up the King of Mog-Mog and his daughter, both injured by shrapnel in the bombardment. When the invasion forces arrived three days later, they found the islands already well occupied. In the Palau operations, 12 September 1944, *Noa* was rammed by DD *Fullam*, a ship twice *Noa's* size, and started to settle. After abandoning ship, *Noa's* skipper led a salvage party back aboard but had to give up after a four-hour battle as the old ship sank by the stern, fortunately

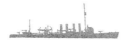

The Stringham (APD-6) in May 1943 after repairs made necessary by a grounding in the Solomons. Two tall stacks still dominate her silhouette, but she has acquired 3-inch guns in place of her old 4-inchers. Radar by this time was a commonplace even for small ships. She and the Manley were the only two of the original six APDs to survive the war.

By January 1945 the Stringham's stacks had been shortened, a pair of 40-mm. guns, mounted singly, replaced the 3-inch gun on the after deckhouse, and some of the depth charges had been replaced by additional 20-mm. guns. Her paint had become bizarre and her numbers had grown big in deference to the need for easy recognition.

with no casualties. Near-disaster struck *Clemson* and *Stringham* at Manus on 3 October, when fire, starting on *Clemson*, spread to rubber boats and sacks of demolition explosive on *Stringham's* deck. Several lives were lost before the fires were put out, and *Stringham* had to go back to the yard for repairs. A week later, *Schley* had her wildcat and anchor engine shaft ripped out while trying to anchor in the face of a strong wind and current in Leyte Gulf, where she was putting Rangers ashore in advance of the main landings. In another unusual accident, *Talbot*, moored at Manus on 10 November of the same year, suddenly found herself on the receiving end of 631 pounds of scrap metal when the ammunition ship *Mount Hood*, berthed 800 yards away, blew up leaving not a single survivor.

By this time, the kamikaze planes were coming into prominence as the prime menace to the U. S. Navy, and APDs off Leyte were among their early targets. *Ward*, exactly three years to the day after she sank the midget submarine at the entrance to Pearl Harbor, took a bomber in her troop spaces and fire room. One of the plane's engines passed completely through the ship and out the other side. Smoke and fire soon cut off all access to the after part of the ship, and efforts to fight the fire from landing craft alongside were futile. As the fire licked towards the magazines and fuel tanks, all hands cleared out, and the derelict was sunk by gunfire from the destroyer *O'Brien*. Skipper of the *O'Brien* was Commander W. W. Outerbridge, the officer who had stood on *Ward's* bridge on Pearl Harbor morning. In the same area on 6 January 1945, *Brooks* was crashed by a Japanese plane in her port side and had to be towed all the way back to San Diego, where she was stripped of her useful parts and decommissioned. *Belknap* similarly became a constructive total loss on 12 January when a Japanese kamikaze plunged into her after stack. Although her hull remained intact, she was completely immobilized and had to be towed to Manus. Eventually able to limp back to the West Coast, she too was surveyed and ultimately sold for scrap.

As the fighting moved north, casualties continued. Before her last fight, *Dickerson* had the unusual experience of hauling a load of Japanese and Korean prisoners from Iwo Jima to Leyte. While the abject captives apologized humbly in advance for any inconvenience they might cause because of

seasickness, the crew noted that one of them carried a current issue of *Esquire* magazine, three months newer than the latest they themselves had on board! After her return to Okinawa, on 2 April 1945, a desperate kamikaze made a sneak approach from directly astern where most of *Dickerson's* battery could not reach him, clipped off both stacks and the foremast, and landed at the base of the bridge. Simultaneously another plane hit her forecastle with a 500-pound bomb that laid the whole deck wide open. Fires soon forced the crew to abandon ship, but the flames later burned down and the smoldering hulk was towed to Kerama Retto. Too far gone for even this graveyard, she was towed to sea and scuttled two days later. Fifty-one officers and men, including the commanding officer, died in her final ordeal.

Rathburne, hit a few weeks later, was luckier. A Japanese seeking glory went right through her bow at the hull numbers, yet not a man was lost. The ship, temporarily patched, headed for home, out of the war. *Stringham*, nearing the end of three years of combat duty, became the unintended victim of the crippled *Fletcher*-class DD *Lavallette*, which rammed her in Apra Harbor, Guam, on 7 May. She too was sent home for repairs. Other kamikaze victims in the final months of the war were *Roper*, damaged and forced to retire, and *Barry*, burned out and abandoned, both on 25 May 1945. *Barry* was reboarded by a skeleton crew and towed to Kerama Retto the next day, but was too far gone to be worth the effort of salvaging. Stripped of all useful gear, her hulk was towed out to sea on 21 June. Even this useless wreck was not spared by the fanatic Japanese, one of whom plunged into her, finally sending her to the bottom, while a companion plane crashed into her escort, *LSM-59*, and sank her as well.

With the war in its final stage, the old flush-deck APDs were, for the most part, shifted to duties in the rear, as newly converted DE types became available to take over their transport chores. Of those sent back home in mid-1945, some were surveyed and decommissioned as worn-out, while others were given back their DD numbers and put to miscellaneous uses similar to the AGs. *Manley*, for example, ending her days as she began, as DD-74, was fitted with a catapult for target drones and operated with other ships to familiarize them with kamikaze tactics. Peace found a few of them still in the Far

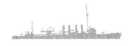

East, serving as convoy escorts and evacuation transports for former POWs. *Gilmer* helped lift units of the Chinese Army to northern ports before departing for home in late November 1945. As for *Greene*, she was one of the unfortunates caught at Buckner Bay by the Okinawa typhoons, and on 9 October was blown high and dry on the beach where her hulk was decommissioned and abandoned.

As a postscript to the typhoons and kamikazes of Okinawa, claim to the wreckage of the brave ships lost there was donated to the Ryukyus government in 1957 for whatever salvage value could be derived from them.

A forlorn and humble end was in store for 35 former DDs, DMs, and DMSs that were reclassified Miscellaneous Auxiliaries (AG) in the waning months of the war. The author of this program must have been wholly devoid of feeling for the historical role these ships had played. Stripped of their armament except for an odd gun or two, these war-weary ships were relegated to home front duties, such as acting as targets for training submarines and aircraft, photography and target-towing missions, plane guards for carriers engaged in shaking down and qualifying their new pilots, testing experimental equipment, and performing similar utilitarian chores.

More honorable was the fate of those destroyers that were lost in action or worn-out in service to the point where they had to be stricken and designated for scrapping even before the war ended—at least they were destroyers to the end. Of the 28 World-War-II flush deckers that never bore any other classification, 11 were lost fairly early in the war. The rest ended their days considerably modified from their original appearance. In successive alterations, their stacks were lowered in height, armament was reduced or drastically changed, and many lost their old Number 4 stack. Thus, these ships underwent almost as complete a metamorphosis as those that were converted to auxiliary types.

Save those lost in action, only five wartime flush deckers ended their careers with the four stacks they had been born with—*Bainbridge, Broome, Decatur, Simpson,* and *Semmes,* and of these *Bainbridge* and *Decatur* were gone before the end of the war. The others ended as AGs. *Semmes* undoubtedly was the last four piper on the U. S. Navy's books when she was stricken in July 1946. Four others were the only ones to remain in commission as destroyers on VJ day (not counting those that

were briefly redesignated destroyers after having been converted to other types for most of the war)—*Chew* (DD-106), *Crane* (DD-109), *King* (DD-242), and *Lawrence* (DD-250). Their careers, oddly enough, had been distinguished by little other than routine service. The last of these on the register was *Crane,* decommissioned 14 November 1945 and stricken 19 December. However, prize honors for long and distinguished service should go to two others that shared the distinction of serving their entire careers in continuous active commission as destroyers. These veterans were the Cramp-built *Barker* (DD-213), in commission from 27 December 1919 to 18 July 1945, and *John D. Edwards* (DD-216), from 6 April 1920 to 28 July 1945. *Bulmer,* although reclassified AG-86, outserved all the rest by staying in commission exactly 26 years— 16 August 1920 to 16 August 1946. But for straight longevity (broken by periods out of commission) *Manley* appears to be the winner, as her name remained on the Navy List from October 1917 to November 1945. Last to go was *Hatfield,* on 28 January 1947.

A few Irish pennants remain to be tidied up in this narrative. There is one more name change, for instance. Early in 1945, when it was desired to give the name *Dallas* to a new cruiser, DD-199 of that name belatedly picked up a first name to become *Alexander Dallas* for the last few months of her career.

Back in the late 1930s, three old hulls were left in limbo when their sisters went to the scrap heap; now it is time to go back and follow their checkered careers. *Taylor* (DD-94) was stricken in 1938, but her hull was still on hand when the war started in Europe, and foresighted people kept an eye out for whatever use might be made of it. In July 1940, the Chief of Naval Operations decided that the ex-*Taylor* and ex-*Walker* (DD-163) were ideal candidates for "old hulks for use as targets in connection with the training of damage-control parties." Before this plan could fully be carried out, war intervened; and *Taylor* continued to rust away until, in 1942, *Blakeley* (DD-150) lost her bow to a Nazi torpedo. *Taylor's* moment had arrived. Her bow was quickly sliced off and grafted onto *Blakeley,* just as *Graham's* bow had been fitted onto *Hulbert* 20 years before. Thus, part of *Taylor* finally got to war. What was left of her was sold for scrap in 1945.

The other candidate for damage-control training,

Scuttled in dry dock at Soerabaja, Java, when the Japanese overran the Dutch East Indies, the USS Stewart (DD-224) was raised and refitted by her captors for use as a convoy escort. Still afloat at war's end, she was towed home and sunk as a target on 24 May 1946. Upper view shows two F6F Hellcats and an F4U Corsair passing over the hulk as they complete their attack. Lower view shows rockets exploding on either side of the target, which sank soon after.

Walker, had also been stricken in 1938, thoroughly demilitarized, and placed on the register of yard craft as a water barge, YW-57. In this ignominious state she was towed about, hauling water, asphalt, and stores between facilities in the San Diego area. In March 1940, during a dry-docking, her hull was found to be in such good condition that hopes were entertained by officers at the Destroyer Base and in the Bureau of Ships of returning her to service as a destroyer, but to no avail. Reclassified IX-44 in January of 1941, she was even denied her old name and given instead the abominable appellation of DCH-1, an abbreviation of the phrase Damage Control Hulk. Work—which consisted of making a few modifications to fit her for her new role—dragged along slowly and, no doubt, reluctantly. Efforts to change the mind of the Chief of Naval Operations and restore her to destroyer status resulted only in permission to salvage machinery and parts as spares for other ships. This further delayed her assignment until October 1941, at which time she was prepared for tow to Pearl Harbor. Here, it was planned to subject her to one shell or bomb hit per attack, after which repairs would be made by damage-control trainees. Although Washington did not contemplate deliberately sinking the hulk, it was recognized that a strong probability existed that she would sink anyway, out of shame, if nothing else. Arrangements were finally completed for the tow, and the Bureau of Ships officer responsible for her maintenance (Lieutenant Commander R. K. James, later Rear Admiral and Chief of the Bureau of Ships, who had led the unsuccessful fight to make a fighting ship out of her once more) wrote: "Things are finally happening to ex-*Walker*." How prophetic these words were became apparent after Pearl Harbor went up in flames on 7 December 1941. When the situation had calmed down a bit, people remembered the DCH-1 again. A frantic message to ComDesBase, San Diego, on 19 December directed: "ADVISE WHEREABOUTS IX-44." Unfortunately, the hulk was already far out in the Pacific. There, a liability to her unarmed tug, and no longer needed to train damage-control parties who had more than enough of the real thing to contend with, she was scuttled ignobly on 28 December to avoid Japanese submarines which were imagined to infest the area.

A happier ending was in store for the third ex-DD, *Turner* (DD-259). Stricken in 1936, she became the unpowered water barge YW-56 and served faithfully between San Diego and San Clemente Island until 1942 when BuShips, searching the musty corners of its establishment for ASW ships, asked the Destroyer Base for its recommendations concerning her employment. The reply was discouraging: "In complying with the provisions of the London Treaty, the ex-*Turner* was placed in non-combatant state by generous use of the oxy-acetylene torch. The propeller struts were burned off about two feet from the shell, all the turbines were burned through in the vicinity of the bearings . . ." The district commandant cast more cold water on plans for restoring the ship to combat duty but, pointing out the real need for a self-propelled water, cargo, and passenger ferry vessel to support the training base at San Clemente, recommended reactivation of the power plant for this purpose and secondarily for duty as a sound school vessel. The Bureau of Ships and the Chief of Naval Operations concurred. The rather jolly name *Moosehead* and classification IX-98 were assigned, a complement of four officers and 60 men was established, and an armament of two 4-inch/50 guns and some light machine guns and depth-charge-throwers was authorized. Now the fun began. Despite the ship's discouraging condition, the Destroyer Base had been waiting for the opportunity to work on her, since the last of the reactivated destroyers had left "red lead row."

Moosehead began to grow. The boilers were retubed, turbines repaired, and the forward fire room stripped to make a cargo hold. Ideas of installing torpedo tubes were firmly squelched by Washington, but the ship's mission was expanded to include training armed guard crews and towing high-speed target sleds. Because of difficulties in getting the damaged intermediate-stage turbine back into operation, this stage was bypassed completely and speed restricted to 21 knots on two boilers. During this time, the Bureau of Ships was crying for information as to just what the Destroyer Base was doing to the ship and insisting on an inclining experiment. Finally the data was forwarded—and promptly hit the fan! "The ship that ComDesBase designed" lacked adequate strength and stability, and the Bureau refused to certify her safety at sea. Off came the guns, extra stiffeners went in around the big cargo hatch, certain water tanks were blanked off, and bulkheads were installed; finally *Moosehead* was given clearance to operate. Commissioned 5 April 1943, under Lieutenant D. J. Spahr, her

The Turner, commissioned in 1919 as DD-259, hauled down her pennant three years later and spent 14 years in idleness at San Diego before she was stricken and converted into the unnamed water barge YW-56 (top picture). When war came, her engines were repaired and she was recommissioned in February 1943 as USS Moosehead (IX 98). Center view shows her at San Diego shortly before recommissioning. Her 4-inch guns had to be removed to reduce weight topside before the ship could be certified as seaworthy. The cargo boom served a hold in what had once been a fire room. Bottom view shows Moosehead at a later stage, with an array of radar and other electronic antennas, and a pair of 3-inch guns, in her role as a CIC training ship. The top photograph is by Ted Stone, middle by Lieutenant Commander D. J. Spahr, bottom by Captain W. D. Acker.

growth was by no means at an end. In fact, it had hardly begun, for *Moosehead* now fell under the eye of Admiral F. C. Denebrink, Commander Operational Training Command Pacific Fleet. This dynamic officer had resolved that the mistakes made in the Solomons battles should never be repeated, and *Moosehead* was the vehicle by which he proposed to bring fleet combat training to the requisite pitch. Accordingly, he made her his flagship—to be a flagship was an honor apparently held by no other flush decker in World War II—and refitted her to his own requirements. The former Number 1 fire room, which had been converted to a cargo hold, was converted again, into a CIC and living quarters; the intermediate-stage turbine was re-activated; electronic equipment was added—radars, VHF fighter director radio, fire-control gear, electronic countermeasures equipment, a new deckhouse for the countermeasures, then more equipment to go into the deckhouse. Two 3-inch/50 guns were put aboard. The Bureau of Ships turned down requests for higher-powered electric generators, a heavier towing winch, and fire-control radar. Still *Moosehead* wouldn't stop growing. The crew increased to six officers and 86 enlisted men. In desperation, the Bureau asked the Chief of Naval Operations to clarify the ship's mission, pointing out hopefully, but futilely, that she could still be converted into a fine fast transport. Finally, another inclining experiment was called for—BuShips simply could not keep up with *Moosehead*'s growth! Thus it was that the ex-*Turner* served out the war training thousands of officers and men for combat duty and at the same time performing a multiplicity of local chores. With justifiable pride her second skipper, Lieutenant Commander W. D. Acker, USNR, described her capabilities:

"We had on the *Moosehead* more radar than any battleship or carrier in the Fleet. Not only that but we had the latest RCM gear in a special house built above the old Number 1 fireroom where most of the CIC training was conducted. At one time we had seven PhDs assigned to the ship just to keep up with the black boxes. We could literally do anything without looking, come in and go out of port in a fog, visibility never worried us. Conduct amphibious landings acting as command ship—night bombardment on San Clemente Island. We trained whole air groups on newly commissioned carriers, at the same time shook the ship down from A to Z. We could

perform every exercise in the tactical pub for every ship in the Navy except mine sweeping. The *Moosehead* was equipped with high speed towing gear and we pulled radar sleds at 30 kts for the cruisers, we retrieved torpedoes for DD's and in fact performed many exercises and developed tactics that weren't even in the book—Admiral Denebrink had a genius for this.

"The *Moosehead* probably conducted the first high speed refueling operation at sea. This was done successfully in excess of 25 kts. . . . The *Moosehead* was probably the first ship to seal the CO in the pilot house and have him take the conn from a fix at sea, find the channel, negotiate the harbor of a busy port and dock the ship without any prompting from any one except CIC. This was done solely on radar information. . . .

"For the record the *Moosehead* had her combat orders to join the fleet when the going got rough at Okinawa and the ship was placed on 24 hours notice . . . but the bombs were dropped and that never came off. . . . None of the ideas originated there, or the tactics developed there were lost and they have become the radar picket ships and the command and communication ships of today. All the officers and men of the IX-98 are proud to have been a part of her."

Moosehead was still growing when the war ended. Efforts to keep this useful craft in service were overruled, and in late 1945 she was ordered to ComEleven for disposal. Decommissioned 19 March 1946, she was stricken from the rolls for the second and last time a month later, having outlived all but a few of her original destroyer sisters.

In 1945 a ghost from the former ranks of the flush deckers made a startling reappearance. Back in 1942, *Stewart* (DD-224) had been scuttled in dry dock at Soerabaja, Java, and abandoned to the oncoming Japanese, who captured the city on 2 March 1942. *Stewart* was duly stricken from the register of naval vessels and her name was assigned to a new DE being constructed in the States.

Off and on during the war, American airmen reported fleeting sightings of a strange-looking warship far behind the Japanese lines, but it was not until the end of the war that the stranger was identified as the former *Stewart* when the unmistakable lines of a flush decker turned up among the remnants of the Nipponese fleet at Kure. The durable

The banana carrier Teapa, formerly the USS Putnam (DD-287), at Miami, Florida. Sold in 1930 for use as a banana boat, she served as an Army cargo carrier and training ship in World War II, and returned to the banana trade after the war. When scrapped in 1955, she probably was the last of the flush-deck, four-pipers still afloat. Photograph by McCormick Shipping Corp.

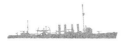

The Tabasco, formerly the USS Worden (DD-288), after her conversion to a banana carrier in 1931. The flag she flew was that of Nicaragua. Two years after her conversion she was wrecked on a reef in the Gulf of Mexico. Photograph by courtesy of F. D. Powers.

wreck, after a year under water, had been floated and patched up by the thrifty enemy and commissioned in their own fleet as *Patrol Vessel (Shokai-tei) No. 102*. Numerous changes had been made in her internal arrangements. All of her U. S. guns and torpedo tubes were removed and in their places were mounted two 75mm. guns of Dutch Army model and two 12.9mm. machine guns. She had been given a distinctively oriental tripod foremast and a trunked stack replacing the old Number 1 and Number 2 smokepipes. According to Japanese sources, this was done to prevent confusing her with U. S. destroyers. These sources also state that "by wonderful skill of her crew she had accomplished her duties" despite her age, obsolescence, and decrepit state. As a patrol and escort ship with the Second South Pacific Fleet, it was claimed, she sank or damaged "several Allied subs." (This claim is not substantiated by any known records.) After a year of duty out of Soerabaja, she was brought to Kure, Japan, in November 1944, and rearmed with two 8cm. antiaircraft guns, four twin and eight single-mount 25mm. machine guns, and 72 depth charges. With only three boilers in operating condition, she was rated as good for 26 knots. After a few more convoy runs she was kept in port at Kure until she was decommissioned on 5 October 1945.

After the surrender of Japan, the unfortunate ship was sailed to Hiro Wan, where, on 29 October 1945, she was recommissioned in the U. S. Navy. Apparently those in charge thought she was supposed to get her old name back, because after the commissioning the Chief of Naval Operations felt impelled to send a dispatch directing that she be known simply as DD-224. The pick-up crew assigned to bring her home had a better name—they called her RAMP-224, standing for Recovered Allied Military Personnel. The trip home was a nightmare of machinery breakdowns, and she finally came through the Golden Gate on the end of a towline. Although the crew had cleaned up the ship, except for several compartments that were left in their Japanese condition, in anticipation of using the vessel as a showpiece, this idea came to naught, and she was finally decommissioned, stricken, and buried at sea on 23 May 1946.

The roster of the flush deckers in the U. S. Navy was closed when *Hatfield* was stricken in 1947, but the class was still not dead. Most of the 50 trans-

ferred to the United Kingdom in 1940 had been sunk or scrapped by this time, but eight survivors of the nine loaned to Russia straggled back to British ports between 1949 and 1952. It appears quite likely that the last flush decker to sail the seas under her own power may have done so under the Soviet flag. The last two, however, *Druzhny* (ex-*Lincoln*, ex-*Yarnall*) which had been thought expended by the Russians for spare parts to keep the others going, and *Doblestny* (ex-*Georgetown*, ex-*Maddox*), were towed back by a British tug, and their ancient bones promptly reduced to scrap.

But even this does not end the story. To pick up the final threads, we have to go back to 1930 when *Putnam* (DD-287), *Worden* (DD-288), *Dale* (DD-290), and *Osborne* (DD-295) were sold for scrap. The owners stripped them to mere shells and converted the hulls into banana carriers for the Standard Fruit Company of New Orleans. Renamed *Teapa*, *Tabasco*, *Masaya*, and *Matagalpa*, respectively, they were given new deckhouses and two 750 h.p. diesel engines and set to work hauling bananas between New Orleans and Central American ports, where their shallow draft enabled them to go up the rivers to the plantations, thus eliminating rail transportation. (See *U. S. Naval Institute Proceedings*, November 1931, and *Our Navy*, Mid-June 1940.) Manned by a crew of only 19 men, they could carry some 25,000 stems of fruit per trip. With both engines full out, their speed of 16 knots made refrigeration unnecessary; instead, a large flow of air was forced into the holds through big windsails. Concerning their employment, a letter from Captain H. C. Laker states: ". . . because of their sharp lines they rolled heavily in a beam sea, but made excellent speed in a head sea, and were always on schedule. I served as Master of the *Matagalpa* for two years, and became quite attached to the ship. . . . the old Commander of her in Navy days often visited us in Norfolk."

Tabasco piled up on Alacran Reef in the Gulf of Mexico in 1933, but the others toiled away unnoticed until World War II. When the situation on Corregidor became desperate early in 1942, General MacArthur pleaded that aid be sent by means of blockade runners directly from the United States. In the quest for suitable vessels, the three banana boats attracted the personal attention of General Brehon B. Somervell (Chief of Transportation, U. S. Army), General Marshall, and President Roosevelt.

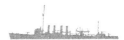

Taken over as U. S. Army Transports on bareboat charter, they were given Army gun crews to man a motley array of armament, and loaded with supplies of the highest priority. *Masaya* left New Orleans on 3 March for Corregidor, via the Panama Canal, Los Angeles, and Honolulu, with a cargo of ammunition, avgas, medical supplies, and mail. Too late to help the garrison of the beleaguered fortress, she was still in Honolulu when the surrender of the Philippines caused her to be diverted to Australia where she was re-manned with an Aussie crew as an inter-island transport for General MacArthur. On 28 March 1943 she was jumped by five Japanese dive bombers and sunk at Oro Bay, New Guinea, with the loss of two lives.

Matagalpa also shoved off with a load of rifles, machine guns, mortars, antitank mines, ammunition, serum, and cigarettes, and she, too, was diverted to the Southwest Pacific. Soon after arriving at Sydney, Australia, she was gutted by fire at her wharf on 27 June 1942, and subsequently scrapped.

Only *Teapa* survived the war. She, too, had left New Orleans for Pearl Harbor but was held up there for engine repairs and ultimately went to Seattle to join the Alaska run. Departing Puget Sound with a cargo of beans, sugar, canned pineapple, cornstarch, and U. S. mail, she lay off Seward, Alaska, until pier space could be made available. While at anchor in Thumb Cove, Resurrection Bay, fire caused by oil from a leaking donkey boiler broke out in Number 3 hold on 28 November 1942. When the flames were finally extinguished by Army and Navy fire-fighting teams from Seward, her decks and wiring were found to be severely damaged. In fact, the deck plates and frames were reported to be so badly corroded that patches could not be welded on safely. Since she was obviously in no shape for further service on the rough Alaska freight route, it was decided to refit her for limited use as a training ship at the Seattle Port of Embarkation. In September 1943 her employment was described as follows:

"Enlisted men in groups of 21 are stationed aboard the *Teapa* for three-week courses in diesel engine operation. Civilians are assigned to the *Teapa* in groups of ten for three-week courses in deck work. Gunnery training consists of instruction and practical firing with a 3-inch/50 gun and a 20mm. antiaircraft gun. The 3-inch/50 is used with a target towed by a Navy minesweeper, and also for antiaircraft drill with a sleeve target towed by a Navy plane.

"On gunnery cruises, which are made twice a week to an area off Port Angeles in the Strait of Juan de Fuca, the *Teapa* carries 25 Navy personnel and 20 Army enlisted men assigned to this port by the Alaska Defense Command for training in vessel operation. This personnel is in addition to those manning the vessel, who for the most part are in training also. Three of the Navy men are instructors, the remainder are gun crews men from transports and merchant ships.

"The Thirteenth Naval District is well pleased with the joint use being made of this vessel, and has shown the utmost cooperation in working out the program. Guns, ammunition, targets, and gunnery instructors are furnished by the Navy."

Surely an old flush-deck destroyer skipper must have been keeping his eye on her! After serving the Army and Navy so well, *Teapa* was demobilized at the end of the war and sold in 1947 to the McCormick Shipping Corporation, in whose employ she carried more bananas until 1950. The author had the good fortune to watch her unload one evening near the end of her career, and to walk the deck of what was probably the last of the flush deckers. Laid up in 1950, she was sold in 1955 to the United Metal Corporation of Miami, Florida, for scrap.

With the passing of *Teapa*, the saga of the flush deckers apparently came to an end, but perhaps even now one survives as a barge or hulk in some backwater. But deep in their hearts, old destroyermen know that somewhere on the wide reaches of the oceans one of their number still carries on, and when the truth becomes known, she will be seen in full fighting regalia escorting the Flying Dutchman into port when he completes his endless seafaring rounds on Judgment Day.

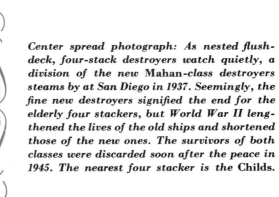

Center spread photograph: As nested flush-deck, four-stack destroyers watch quietly, a division of the new Mahan-class destroyers steams by at San Diego in 1937. Seemingly, the fine new destroyers signified the end for the elderly four stackers, but World War II lengthened the lives of the old ships and shortened those of the new ones. The survivors of both classes were discarded soon after the peace in 1945. The nearest four stacker is the Childs.

Statistical Summary
of the
Flush-Deck Destroyers

GENERAL NOTES

1. Date decommissioned: Only the date of final decommissioning is listed, except where ship was sunk, in which case the date of loss is used.

2. Disposition: Ships listed as "sold, scrapped" were sold to scrap dealers and are presumed to have been scrapped. Those listed as "scrapped, sold" were scrapped by the Navy and their materials sold. Those listed as "hulk" were demilitarized and when last reported had been reduced to hulks; in the absence of other information, they are presumed to have been scrapped by this time.

3. Renaming: When ships were renamed before commissioning, the earlier name is given in parentheses to indicate that the ship never served under that name.

4. Reclassification of DM-1 through 14: As early as 18 March 1920, these ships were designated for conversion to light minelayers, but DM numbers were not assigned until the present classification system was promulgated. The ships were first listed with DM numbers in the 1920 issue of *Ships' Data U.S. Naval Vessels*, dated 1 July 1920. This publication antedated the standard nomenclature system officially established with the issue of General Order No. 541 dated 17 July 1920, which date is used as the official reclassification date. Conversion of the individual

ships was accomplished during 1920 and 1921. Considerable confusion continued to exist regarding the status of these ships until SecNav in a letter dated 15 March 1921 stated as policy that "the following destroyers be considered permanently designated as light minelayers," listing all 14 by name but not by number. The ships continued for years to use their DD numbers in ships' logs, official correspondence, and on the bows of the ships themselves.

5. Transfers to the United Kingdom: British usage does not correspond exactly to U.S. practice. In general, the term "paid off" is considered equivalent to decommissioning, but there is no British action corresponding to striking of vessels from the register. "Breaking up" is, of course, equivalent to scrapping. British ships were reduced to various categories in reserve; the dates listed are the earliest obtainable from Admiralty sources, but these records were not necessarily complete. Various of the British "Town" class were transferred between Allied navies (Canadian, Norwegian, Polish) with varying degrees of formality such as loan, manning, or outright transfer. Not all of these loans are listed in the summary because they were more in the nature of operational assignments than complete transfers.

The **Kimberly** *(DD-80) screening the transport USS Leviathan in the North Atlantic in World War I, from a painting by Burnell Poole. Very few of the flush deckers were completed in time to take an active part in that war.*

No.	Name	1st Comm.	Decomm.	Disposition
69	Caldwell	1 Dec 17	27 Jun 22	Stricken 7 Jan 36, sold, scrapped.
70	Craven	19 Oct 18	15 Jun 22	Name dropped 31 May 35.
	DD-70			Renamed *Conway* 30 Nov 39.
	Conway	8 Aug 40	23 Oct 40	Transferred to UK 23 Oct 40.
	HMS *Lewes*	23 Oct 40		Assigned as target ship and tender Mar 43. Paid off in Australia 45. Sold for scrap 46.
71	Gwin	18 Mar 20	28 Jun 22	Stricken 25 Jan 37, sold, hulk.
72	Conner	12 Jan 18	23 Oct 40	Transferred to UK 23 Oct 40.
	HMS *Leeds*	23 Oct 40	10 Apr 45	Paid off 10 Apr 45. Broken up 48.
73	Stockton	26 Nov 17	23 Oct 40	Transferred to UK 23 Oct 40.
	HMS *Ludlow*	23 Oct 40		Placed in reserve Jun 45. Broken up 45.
74	Manley	15 Oct 17	19 Nov 45	Reclassified AG-28 28 Nov 38. Reclassified APD-1 2 Aug 40. Reclassified DD-74 25 Jun 45. Stricken 5 Dec 45, sold, scrapped.
75	Wickes	31 Jul 18	23 Oct 40	Transferred to UK 23 Oct 40.
	HMS *Montgomery*	23 Oct 40		Placed in reserve 23 Feb 44. Broken up 45.
76	Philip	24 Aug 18	23 Oct 40	Transferred to UK 23 Oct 40.
	HMS *Lancaster*	23 Oct 40	30 Jun 45	Assigned as aircraft training ship Mar 45. Paid off 30 Jun 45. Placed in reserve 3 Jul 45. Broken up 47.
77	Woolsey	30 Sep 18	26 Feb 21	Rammed and sunk by SS *Steel Inventor* off Panama 26 Feb 21.
78	Evans	11 Nov 18	23 Oct 40	Transferred to UK 23 Oct 40.
	HMS *Mansfield*	23 Oct 40	12 Oct 43	Loaned to RNorN Dec 40 to 20 Mar 42. Paid off 12 Oct 43 and placed in reserve in Canada. Sold for scrap 21 Oct 44. Towed to US for scrapping Apr 45.
79	Little	6 Apr 18	5 Sep 42	Reclassified APD-4 2 Aug 40. Sunk by Japanese destroyers *Yudachi, Hatsuyuki & Murakumo* off Guadalcanal 5 Sep 42.
80	Kimberly	26 Apr 18	30 Jun 22	Stricken 25 Jan 37, sold, hulk.

No.	Name	1st Comm.	Decomm.	Disposition
81	Sigourney	15 May 18	26 Nov 40	Transferred to UK 26 Nov 40.
	HMS Newport	5 Dec 40		Loaned to RNorN Mar 41 to Jun 42. Assigned as aircraft training ship 45. Placed in reserve 8 Jul 45. Broken up 47.
82	Gregory	1 Jun 18	5 Sep 42	Reclassified APD-3 2 Aug 40. Sunk by Japanese destroyers Yudachi, Hatsuyuki & Murakumo off Guadalcanal 5 Sep 42.
83	Stringham	2 Jul 18	9 Nov 45	Reclassified APD-6 2 Aug 40. Reclassified DD-83 25 Jun 45. Stricken 5 Dec 45, scrapped.
84	Dyer	1 Jul 18	7 Jun 32	Stricken 7 Jan 36, sold, hulk.
85	Colhoun	13 Jun 18	30 Aug 42	Reclassified APD-2 2 Aug 40. Sunk by Japanese aircraft off Guadalcanal 30 Aug 42.
86	Stevens	24 May 18	19 Jun 22	Stricken 7 Jan 36, sold, hulk.
87	McKee	7 Sep 18	16 Jun 22	Stricken 7 Jan 36, sold, hulk.
88	Robinson	19 Oct 18	26 Nov 40	Transferred to UK 26 Nov 40.
	HMS Newmarket	5 Dec 40	4 Jul 45	Assigned as aircraft training ship 44. Paid off and placed in reserve 4 Jul 45. Broken up 46.
89	Ringgold	14 Nov 18	26 Nov 40	Transferred to UK 26 Nov 40.
	HMS Newark	5 Dec 40		Paid off as DD and assigned as aircraft training ship 28 Dec 44. Broken up 47.
90	McKean	25 Feb 19	17 Nov 43	Reclassified APD-5 2 Aug 40. Sunk by Japanese torpedo aircraft off Bougainville 17 Nov 43.
91	Harding	24 Jan 19	1 Jul 22	Stricken 7 Jan 36, sold, hulk.
92	Gridley	8 Mar 19	22 Jun 22	Name dropped 31 May 35.
	DD-92			Stricken 25 Jan 37, sold, hulk.
93	Fairfax	6 Apr 18	26 Nov 40	Transferred to UK 26 Nov 40.
	HMS Richmond	5 Dec 40	16 Jul 44	Transferred to USSR 16 Jul 44.
	Zhivuchi (USSR)	16 Jul 44	23 Jun 49	Returned to UK 23 Jun 49. Broken up 49.
94	Taylor	1 Jun 18	23 Sep 38	Stricken 6 Dec 38. Designated for use as Damage Control Hulk, 40. Bow used to repair Blakeley (DD-150) 42. Remains sold for scrap 8 Aug 45.
95	Bell	31 Jul 18	21 Jun 22	Stricken 25 Jan 37, sold, hulk.
96	Stribling	16 Aug 18	26 Jul 22	Reclassified DM-1 17 Jul 20. Stricken 1 Dec 36. Sunk as target off Pearl Harbor 28 Jul 37.
97	Murray	21 Aug 18	1 Jul 22	Reclassified DM-2 17 Jul 20. Stricken 7 Jan 36, sold, scrapped.
98	Israel	13 Sep 18	7 Jul 22	Reclassified DM-3 17 Jul 20. Stricken 25 Jan 37, sold, hulk.
99	Luce (ex-Schley)	11 Sep 18	31 Jan 31	Renamed 4 Dec 17. Reclassified DM-4 17 Jul 20. Stricken 7 Jan 36, sold, scrapped.
100	Maury	23 Sep 18	19 Mar 30	Reclassified DM-5 17 Jul 20. Stricken 22 Oct 30, sold, scrapped.
101	Lansdale	26 Oct 18	24 Mar 31	Reclassified DM-6 17 Jul 20. Stricken 25 Jan 37, sold, hulk.
102	Mahan	24 Oct 18	1 May 30	Reclassified DM-7 17 Jul 20. Stricken 22 Oct 30, sold.
103	Schley	20 Sep 18	9 Nov 45	Reclassified APD-14 2 Jan 43. Reclassified DD-103 5 Jul 45. Stricken 5 Dec 45, scrapped.
104	Champlin	11 Nov 18	7 Jun 22	Stricken 19 May 36. Sunk as target off San Diego 12 Aug 36.
105	Mugford	25 Nov 18	7 Jun 22	Name dropped 31 May 35.
	DD-105			Stricken 19 May 36, sold, scrapped.
106	Chew	12 Dec 18	10 Oct 45	Stricken 1 Nov 45, sold, scrapped.
107	Hazelwood	20 Feb 19	15 Nov 30	Designated "Light Target #2" (IX-36) 5 Nov 30. Name and classification restored 11 Aug 31. Stricken 5 Jun 35, sold, scrapped.
108	Williams	1 Mar 19	24 Sep 40	Transferred to UK 24 Sep 40.
	HMS St. Clair	24 Sep 40	Aug 44	Paid off Aug 44. Assigned as fire-fighting training hulk until 45. Disposed of for scrapping 6 Oct 46. Sank while under tow.

This is the stern of the Manley (DD-74) after she was placed in a British dry dock following the explosion of her depth charges in March 1918. It was a bad beginning to a great career which was to last longer than that of any of the other flush-deck four-pipers.

No.	Name	1st Comm.	Decomm.	Disposition
109	Crane	18 Apr 19	14 Nov 45	Stricken 19 Dec 45, sold, scrapped.
110	Hart	26 May 19	1 Jun 31	Reclassified DM-8 17 Jul 20. Stricken 11 Nov 31, scrapped, sold.
111	Ingraham	15 May 19	29 Jun 22	Reclassified DM-9 17 Jul 20. Stricken 1 Dec 36. Sunk as target off Pearl Harbor 23 Jul 37.
112	Ludlow	23 Dec 18	24 May 30	Reclassified DM-10 17 Jul 20. Stricken 18 Nov 30, scrapped, sold.
113	Rathburne	24 Jun 18	2 Nov 45	Reclassified APD-25 20 May 44. Reclassified DD-113 20 Jun 45. Stricken 28 Nov 45, sold, scrapped.
114	Talbot	20 Jul 18	9 Oct 45	Reclassified APD-7 31 Oct 42. Reclassified DD-114 16 Jul 45. Stricken 24 Oct 45, sold, scrapped.
115	Waters	6 Aug 18	12 Oct 45	Reclassified APD-8 31 Oct 42. Reclassified DD-115 2 Aug 45. Stricken 24 Oct 45, sold, scrapped.
116	Dent	9 Sep 18	4 Dec 45	Reclassified APD-9 31 Oct 42. Stricken 3 Jan 46, sold, scrapped.
117	Dorsey	16 Sep 18	8 Dec 45	Reclassified DMS-1 19 Nov 40. Grounded in typhoon at Okinawa 9 Oct 45, total loss. Stricken 3 Jan 46.
118	Lea	2 Oct 18	20 Jul 45	Stricken 13 Aug 45, sold, scrapped.
119	Lamberton	22 Aug 18	13 Dec 46	Reclassified AG-21 16 Apr 32. Reclassified DMS-2 19 Nov 40. Reclassified AG-21 5 May 45. Stricken 28 Jan 47, sold, scrapped.
120	Radford	30 Sep 18	9 Jun 22	Reclassified AG-22 16 Apr. 32. Reclassified DD-120 27 Jun 32. Stricken 19 May 36, sunk as target off San Diego 5 Aug 36.
121	Montgomery	26 Jul 18	23 Apr 45	Reclassified DM-17 5 Jan 31. Damaged by mine at Ngulu Lagoon, South Pacific 17 Oct 44, beyond repair. Stricken 28 Apr 45, sold, scrapped.
122	Breese	23 Oct 18	15 Jan 46	Reclassified DM-18 5 Jan 31. Stricken 7 Feb 46, sold, scrapped.
123	Gamble	29 Nov 18	1 Jun 45	Reclassified DM-15 13 Jun 30. Damaged by Japanese aircraft at Iwo Jima 17 Feb 45, beyond repair. Scuttled off Saipan 16 Jul 45.
124	Ramsay	15 Feb 19	19 Oct 45	Reclassified DM-16 13 Jun 30. Reclassified AG-98 5 Jun 45. Stricken 13 Nov 45, sold, scrapped.
125	Tattnall	26 Jun 19	17 Dec 45	Reclassified APD-19 24 Jul 43. Stricken 8 Jan 46, sold, scrapped.
126	Badger	29 May 19	20 Jul 45	Stricken 13 Aug 45, sold, scrapped.
127	Twiggs	28 Jul 19	23 Oct 40	Transferred to UK 23 Oct 40.
	HMS Leamington	23 Oct 40	16 Jul 44	Transferred to USSR 16 Jul 44.
	Zhguchi (USSR)	16 Jul 44	30 Jan 50	Returned to UK 30 Jan 50. Broken up 52.
128	Babbitt	24 Oct 19	25 Jan 46	Reclassified AG-102 10 Jun 45. Stricken 25 Feb 46, sold, scrapped.
129	De Long	20 Sep 19	17 Mar 22	Grounded Half Moon Bay, Calif., 1 Dec 21. Salved. Stricken and sold 25 Sep 22, scrapped.
130	Jacob Jones	20 Oct 19	28 Feb 42	Sunk by German submarine U-578 off Delaware Capes 28 Feb 42.
131	Buchanan	20 Jan 19	9 Sep 40	Transferred to UK 9 Sep 40.
	HMS Campbeltown	9 Sep 40	28 Mar 42	Manned by Polish Navy 41. Blown up as blockship at St. Nazaire 28 Mar 42.
132	Aaron Ward	21 Apr 19	9 Sep 40	Transferred to UK 9 Sep 40.
	HMS Castleton	9 Sep 40		Placed in reserve 13 Mar 45. Broken up 48.

USS Craven full dressed soon after her commissioning in October 1918. Notice the white shadowing on her dark numbers. In 1935, after thirteen years of inactivity, her name was given to a new destroyer in the expectation that this ship would never sail again. When World War II began she was renamed Conway and was recommissioned in August 1940 under that name. Two months later she became HMS Lewes.

Four-pipers were in the Black Sea during the Russian Revolution chiefly to save as many lives as possible. Two of them are visible in this view, taken on 13 October 1920, of an oil tanker burning at Batumi, not far from the Turkish border. Photograph by G. Le Brun.

No.	Name	1st Comm.	Decomm.	Disposition
133	Hale	12 Jun 19	9 Sep 40	Transferred to UK 9 Sep 40.
	HMS Caldwell	9 Sep 40	Dec 43	Placed in reserve 24 Feb 44. Broken up 45.
134	Crowninshield	6 Aug 19	9 Sep 40	Transferred to UK 9 Sep 40.
	HMS Chelsea	9 Sep 40	16 Jul 44	Transferred to USSR 16 Jul 44.
	Dyerzki (USSR)	16 Jul 44	23 Jun 49	Returned to UK 23 Jun 49. Broken up 49.
135	Tillman	30 Apr 21	26 Nov 40	Transferred to UK 26 Nov 40.
	HMS Wells	5 Dec 40		Assigned as aircraft training ship 45. Placed in reserve 24 Jul 45. Broken up 45.
136	Boggs	23 Sep 18	20 Mar 46	Designated "Light Target #2" (IX-36) 11 Aug 31. Reclassified AG-19 5 Sep 31. Reclassified DMS-3 19 Nov 40. Reclassified AG-19 5 Jun 45. Stricken 12 Apr 46, sold, scrapped.
137	Kilty	17 Dec 18	2 Nov 45	Designated "Light Target #3" (IX-37) 11 Aug 31. Reclassified AG-20 5 Sep 31. Reclassified DD-137 16 Apr 32. Reclassified APD-15 2 Jan 43. Reclassified DD-137 20 Jul 45. Stricken 16 Nov 45, sold, scrapped.
138	Kennison	2 Apr 19	23 Nov 45	Reclassified AG-83 1 Oct 44. Stricken 5 Dec 45, sold, scrapped.
139	Ward (ex-Cowell)	24 Jul 18	7 Dec 44	Renamed 20 May 18. Reclassified APD-16 2 Jan 43. Sunk by Japanese suicide aircraft at Ormoc Bay 7 Dec 44.
140	Claxton	13 Sep 19	26 Nov 40	Transferred to UK 26 Nov 40.
	HMS Salisbury	5 Dec 40	10 Dec 43	Paid off 10 Dec 43 and placed in reserve in Canada. Sold for scrap 21 Oct 44. Towed to US for scrapping Apr 45.
141	Hamilton	7 Nov 19	16 Oct 45	Reclassified DMS-18 11 Oct. 41. Reclassified AG-111 5 Jun 44. Stricken 1 Nov 45, sold, scrapped.
142	Tarbell	27 Nov 18	20 Jul 45	Stricken 13 Aug 45, sold, scrapped.
143	Yarnall	29 Nov 18	23 Oct 40	Transferred to UK 23 Oct 40.
	HMS Lincoln	23 Oct 40	26 Aug 44	Loaned to RNorN Feb 42. Transferred to USSR 26 Aug 44 for spare parts.
	Druzhny (USSR)	26 Aug 44	23 Aug 52	Returned to UK 23 Aug 52. Broken up 52.
144	Upshur	23 Dec 18	2 Nov 45	Reclassified AG-103 30 Jun 45. Stricken 16 Nov 45, sold, scrapped.
145	Greer	31 Dec 18	19 Jul 45	Stricken 13 Aug 45, sold, scrapped.
146	Elliot	25 Jan 19	12 Oct 45	Reclassified DMS-4 19 Nov 40. Reclassified AG-104 5 Jun 45. Stricken 24 Oct 45, sold, scrapped.
147	Roper	15 Feb 19	15 Sep 45	Reclassified APD-20 20 Oct 43. Stricken 11 Oct 45, sold, scrapped.
148	Breckinridge	27 Feb 19	30 Nov 45	Reclassified AG-112 30 Jun 45. Stricken 19 Dec 45, sold, scrapped.
149	Barney	14 Mar 19	30 Nov 45	Reclassified AG-113 30 Jun 45. Stricken 19 Dec 45, sold, scrapped.
150	Blakeley	8 May 19	21 Jul 45	Torpedoed by German submarine off Martinique 25 May 42. Repaired with bow from Taylor (DD-94). Stricken 13 Aug 45, sold, scrapped.
151	Biddle	22 Apr 19	5 Oct 45	Reclassified AG-114 30 Jun 45. Stricken 24 Oct 45, sold, scrapped.
152	Du Pont	30 Apr 19	2 May 46	Reclassified AG-80 25 Sep 44. Stricken 5 Jun 46, sold, scrapped.
153	Bernadou	19 May 19	17 Jul 45	Stricken 13 Aug 45, sold, scrapped.
154	Ellis	7 Jun 19	31 Oct 45	Reclassified AG-115 30 Jun 45. Stricken 16 Nov 45, sold, scrapped.
155	Cole	19 Jun 19	1 Nov 45	Reclassified AG-116 30 Jun 45. Stricken 16 Nov 45, sold, scrapped.

Eighty-eight feet above sea level, nine flush deckers transit the Panama Canal on 24 July 1919 en route to join Destroyer Flotilla Four in the Pacific. The nearest destroyer, Yarnall, survived until 1952. The last eight of her 34 years were spent under the Soviet flag.

The Scouting Fleet in Guantanamo Bay in 1920 or 1921. The Harding and a Bird-class minesweeper are in the center, ready to tend aircraft. The four seaplanes in the foreground are Curtiss H-16 twin-engine patrol planes, of which 274 were delivered, beginning in 1918.

Pendragon Books

5560 College Ave · (at OceanView)
Oakland · 94618 Telephone · 652-6259

No.	Name	1st Comm.	Decomm.	Disposition
156	J. Fred Talbott	30 Jun 19	21 May 46	Reclassified AG-81 25 Sep 44. Stricken 19 Jun 46, sold, scrapped.
157	Dickerson	3 Sep 19	4 Apr 45	Reclassified APD-21 21 Aug 43. Damaged by Japanese suicide aircraft at Okinawa 2 Apr 45, beyond repair. Scuttled off Okinawa, 4 Apr 45.
158	Leary	5 Dec 19	24 Dec 43	Sunk by German submarine U-275 in mid-Atlantic 24 Dec 43.
159	Schenck	30 Oct 19	17 May 46	Reclassified AG-82 25 Sep 44. Stricken 5 Jun 46, sold, scrapped.
160	Herbert	21 Nov 19	25 Sep 45	Reclassified APD-22 1 Dec 43. Stricken 24 Oct 45, sold, scrapped.
161	Palmer	22 Nov 18	7 Jan 45	Reclassified DMS-5 19 Nov 40. Sunk by Japanese aircraft in Lingayen Gulf 7 Jan 45.
162	Thatcher	14 Jan 19	24 Sep 40	Transferred to UK 24 Sep 40.
	HMCS Niagara	24 Sep 40	15 Sep 45	Assigned as torpedo firing ship 2 Mar 44. Disposed of for scrapping 27 May 46.
163	Walker	31 Jan 19	7 Jun 22	Stricken 28 Mar 38. Converted to water barge. Reclassified YW-57 30 Mar 39.
	YW-57	30 Mar 39	6 Jan 41	Designated Damage Control Hulk DCH-1 and reclassified IX-44 6 Jan 41.
	DCH-1	6 Jan 41	28 Dec 41	Scuttled mid-Pacific 28 Dec 41.
164	Crosby	24 Jan 19	28 Sep 45	Reclassified APD-17 2 Jan 43. Stricken 24 Oct 45, sold, scrapped.
165	Meredith	29 Jan 19	28 Jun 22	Stricken 7 Jan 36, sold, scrapped.
166	Bush	19 Feb 19	21 Jun 22	Stricken 7 Jan 36, sold, hulk.
167	Cowell	17 Mar 19	23 Sep 40	Transferred to UK 23 Sep 40.
	HMS Brighton	23 Sep 40	16 Jul 44	Assigned as aircraft training ship Nov 42 to Apr 43. Transferred to USSR 16 Jul 44.
	Zharki (USSR)	16 Jul 44	4 Mar 49	Returned to UK 4 Mar 49. Broken up 49.
168	Maddox	10 Mar 19	23 Sep 40	Transferred to UK 23 Sep 40.
	HMS Georgetown	23 Sep 40	10 Aug 44	Transferred to USSR 10 Aug 44.
	Zhyostki (USSR)	10 Aug 44	5 Sep 52	Returned to UK 5 Sep 52. Broken up 52.
169	Foote	21 Mar 19	23 Sep 40	Transferred to UK 23 Sep 40.
	HMS Roxborough	23 Sep 40	10 Aug 44	Transferred to USSR 10 Aug 44.
	Doblestny (USSR)	10 Aug 44	7 Feb 49	Returned to UK 7 Feb 49. Broken up 49.
170	Kalk (ex-Rodgers)	29 Mar 19	23 Sep 40	Renamed 23 Dec 18. Transferred to UK 23 Sep 40.
	HMS Hamilton	23 Sep 40	Oct 40	Damaged by collision and grounding. Transferred to RCN Oct 40.
	HMCS Hamilton	Jun 41	8 Jun 45	Assigned as training tender 11 Aug 43. Sold and towed to US for scrapping Jul 45.
171	Burns	7 Aug 19	2 Jun 30	Reclassified DM-11 17 Jul 20. Stricken 18 Nov 30, used as barracks ship, scrapped and sold 32.
172	Anthony	19 Jun 19	30 Jun 22	Reclassified DM-12 17 Jul 20. Stricken 1 Dec 36, sunk as target off California 22 Jul 37.
173	Sproston	12 Jul 19	15 Aug 22	Reclassified DM-13 17 Jul 20. Stricken 1 Dec 36, sunk as target off California 20 Jul 37.
174	Rizal	28 May 19	20 Aug 31	Reclassified DM-14 17 Jul 20. Stricken 11 Nov 31, scrapped, sold.
175	Mackenzie	25 Jul 19	24 Sep 40	Transferred to UK 24 Sep 40.
	HMCS Annapolis	24 Sep 40	45	Assigned as training vessel Apr 44. Sold 21 Jun 45, towed to US for scrapping.
176	Renshaw	31 Jul 19	27 May 22	Stricken 19 May 36, sold, hulk.
177	O'Bannon	27 Aug 19	27 May 22	Stricken 19 May 36, sold, hulk.
178	Hogan	1 Oct 19	11 Oct 45	Reclassified DMS-6 19 Nov 40. Reclassified AG-105 5 Jun 45. Stricken 1 Nov 45, sunk as target 8 Nov 45 by aircraft bombs off San Diego.

View on pages 70 and 71 shows the Nicholas (311) and the S. P. Lee shortly after they were wrecked at Point Arguello, California, on 8 September 1923 in company with five other flush-deck four-stackers. They were all steaming in column in a fog at 20 knots. Most of the ships in the squadron were relying on the flagship's navigation, and that ship's navigation proved to be in error. The point that each ship should do her own navigation has not been lost on subsequent generations of officers.

Top picture on opposite page was taken over the wreck of the flagship Delphy and shows the overturned Young, with the Woodbury and Fuller beyond. Air view at center left shows Fuller (foreground) with Woodbury just beyond. Nicholas is broadside to the camera at left and S. P. Lee is almost stern-to. Young is capsized just inshore of the Woodbury and the Delphy is in two parts just beyond the Young. Semi-submerged at right is the Chauncey. Center-right photo shows the Chauncey in the foreground. Bottom picture shows the wreck of the Chauncey a few years later. The ships defied all efforts at salvage, and the wrecks were sold in 1925 for 1,035 dollars.

No.	Name	1st Comm.	Decomm.	Disposition
179	Howard	29 Jan 20	30 Nov 45	Reclassified DMS-7 19 Nov 40. Reclassified AG-106 5 Jun 45. Stricken 19 Dec 45, sold, scrapped.
180	Stansbury	8 Jan 20	11 Dec 45	Reclassified DMS-8 19 Nov 40. Reclassified AG-107 5 Jun 45. Stricken 3 Jan 46, sold, scrapped.
181	Hopewell	21 Mar 19	23 Sep 40	Transferred to UK 23 Sep 40.
	HMS Bath	23 Sep 40	19 Aug 41	Transferred to RNorN 1 Jan 41. Sunk by German submarine west of Ushant 19 Aug 41.
182	Thomas	25 Apr 19	23 Sep 40	Transferred to UK 23 Sep 40.
	HMS St. Albans	23 Sep 40	16 Jul 44	Loaned to RNorN 18 Apr 41. Transferred to USSR 16 Jul 44.
	Dostoiny (USSR)	16 Jul 44	4 Mar 49	Returned to UK 4 Mar 49. Broken up 49.
183	Haraden	7 Jun 19	24 Sep 40	Transferred to UK 24 Sep 40.
	HMCS Columbia	24 Sep 40	12 Jun 45	Damaged by running into shore 25 Feb 44. Assigned as fuel and ammunition hulk. Paid off 12 Jun 45. Disposed of 9 Aug 45 and sold for scrapping.
184	Abbot	19 Jul 19	23 Sep 40	Transferred to UK 23 Sep 40.
	HMS Charlestown	23 Sep 40	15 Jan 45	Damaged in collision with SS Florizel off Harwich Dec 44. Paid off and placed in reserve 15 Jan 45. Broken up 48.
185	Bagley	27 Aug 19	12 Jul 22	Name dropped 31 May 35.
	DD-185			Renamed Doran 22 Dec 39.
	Doran	17 Jun 40	23 Sep 40	Transferred to UK 23 Sep 40.
	HMS St. Marys	23 Sep 40	Feb 44	Placed in reserve 6 Sep 44. Broken up 45.
186	Clemson	29 Dec 19	12 Oct 45	Reclassified AVP-17 15 Nov 39. Reclassified AVD-4 2 Aug 40. Reclassified DD-186 1 Dec 43. Reclassified APD-31 7 Mar 44. Reclassified DD-186 16 Jul 45. Stricken 24 Oct 45, sold, scrapped.
187	Dahlgren	6 Jan 20	14 Dec 45	Reclassified AG-91 1 Mar 45. Stricken 8 Jan 46, sold, scrapped.
188	Goldsborough	26 Jan 20	11 Oct 45	Reclassified AVP-18 15 Nov 39. Reclassified AVD-5 2 Aug 40. Reclassified DD-188 1 Dec 43. Reclassified APD-32 7 Mar 44. Reclassified DD-188 10 Jul 45. Stricken 24 Oct 45, sold, scrapped.
189	Semmes	21 Feb 20	21 Jun 46	Transferred to USCG 25 Apr 32. Returned to USN 20 Apr 34. Reclassified AG-24 1 Jul 35. Stricken 3 Jul 46, sold, scrapped.
190	Satterlee	23 Dec 19	8 Oct 40	Transferred to UK 8 Oct 40.
	HMS Belmont	8 Oct 40	31 Jan 42	Sunk by German submarine in North Atlantic 31 Jan 42.
191	Mason	28 Feb 20	8 Oct 40	Transferred to UK 8 Oct 40.
	HMS Broadwater	8 Oct 40	18 Oct 41	Sunk by German submarine U-101 in North Atlantic 18 Oct 41.
192	Graham	13 Mar 20	31 Mar 22	Damaged beyond repair in collision 16 Dec 21. Bow installed on Hulbert (DD-342). Remainder sold for scrap 19 Sep 22.
193	Abel P. Upshur	23 Nov 20	9 Sep 40	Transferred to USCG 5 Nov 30. Returned to USN 21 May 34. Transferred to UK 9 Sep 40.
	HMS Clare	9 Sep 40	16 Aug 45	Converted to convoy escort. Assigned as aircraft training ship May 44. Paid off and placed in reserve 16 Aug 45. Broken up 46.
194	Hunt	30 Sep 20	8 Oct 40	Transferred to USCG 13 Sep 30. Returned to USN 28 May 34. Transferred to UK 8 Oct 40.
	HMS Broadway	8 Oct 40		Assigned as aircraft training ship Sep 43. Placed in reserve 9 Aug 45. Broken up 47.

No.	Name	1st Comm.	Decomm.	Disposition
195	*Welborn C. Wood*	14 Jan 21	9 Sep 40	Transferred to USCG 1 Oct 30. Returned to USN 21 May 34. Transferred to UK 9 Sep 40.
	HMS *Chesterfield*	9 Sep 40		Assigned as aircraft training ship Nov 43. Placed in reserve 15 Jan 45. Broken up 47.
196	*George E. Badger*	28 Jul 20	3 Oct 45	Transferred to USCG 1 Oct 30. Returned to USN 21 May 34. Reclassified AVP-16 1 Oct 39. Reclassified AVD-3 2 Aug 40. Reclassified DD-196 4 Nov 43. Reclassified APD-33 10 Apr 44. Reclassified DD-196 20 Jul 45. Stricken 24 Oct 45, scrapped.
197	*Branch*	26 Jul 20	8 Oct 40	Transferred to UK 8 Oct 40.
	HMS *Beverley*	8 Oct 40	11 Apr 43	Sunk by German submarine in North Atlantic 11 Apr 43.
198	*Herndon*	14 Sep 20	9 Sep 40	Transferred to USCG 13 Sep 30. Returned to USN 28 May 34. Transferred to UK 9 Sep 40.
	HMS *Churchill*	9 Sep 40	16 Jul 44	Transferred to USSR 16 Jul 44.
	Dyeyatelni (USSR)	16 Jul 44	16 Jan 45	Sunk by German submarine off Cape Tereberski 16 Jan 45.
199	*Dallas*	29 Oct 20		Renamed *Alexander Dallas* 31 Mar 45.
	Alexander Dallas		28 Jul 45	Stricken 13 Aug 45, sold, scrapped.
200-205	Contract cancelled, no names assigned			
206	*Chandler*	5 Sep 19	21 Dec 45	Reclassified DMS-9 19 Nov 40. Reclassified AG-108 5 Jun 45. Stricken 5 Dec 45, sold, scrapped.
207	*Southard*	25 Sep 19	15 Dec 45	Reclassified DMS-10 19 Nov 40. Grounded in typhoon at Okinawa 9 Oct 45, total loss. Stricken 8 Jan 46.
208	*Hovey*	2 Oct 19	6 Jan 45	Reclassified DMS-11 19 Nov 40. Sunk by Japanese aircraft in Lingayen Gulf 6 Jan 45.
209	*Long*	20 Oct 19	6 Jan 45	Reclassified DMS-12 19 Nov 40. Sunk by Japanese aircraft off west coast of Luzon 6 Jan 45.
210	*Broome*	31 Oct 19	20 May 46	Reclassified AG-96 23 May 45. Stricken 19 Jun 46, sold, scrapped.
211	*Alden*	24 Nov 19	20 Jul 45	Stricken 13 Aug 45, sold, scrapped.
212	*Smith Thompson*	10 Dec 19	15 May 36	Damaged in collision with *Whipple* (DD-217) 14 Apr 36, beyond repair. Stricken 19 May 36. Scuttled off Subic Bay 25 Jul 36.
213	*Barker*	27 Dec 19	18 Jul 45	Stricken 13 Aug 45, sold, scrapped.
214	*Tracy*	9 Mar 20	16 Jan 46	Reclassified DM-19 30 Jun 37. Stricken 7 Feb 46, sold, scrapped.
215	*Borie*	24 Mar 20	2 Nov 43	Sunk by aircraft from USS *Card* (CVE-11) after damage from ramming German submarine U-405 north of Azores 2 Nov 43.
216	*John D. Edwards* (ex-*Stewart*)	6 Apr 20	28 Jul 45	Renamed 11 Nov 19. Stricken 13 Aug 45, sold, scrapped.
217	*Whipple*	23 Apr 20	9 Nov 45	Reclassified AG-117 30 Jun 45. Stricken 5 Dec 45, scrapped.
218	*Parrott*	11 May 20	16 Jun 44	Rammed by SS *John Morton* at Norfolk, Va. 2 May 44. Beached and salved but beyond repair. Sold for scrap 5 Apr 47.
219	*Edsall*	26 Nov 20	1 Mar 42	Sunk by gunfire of Japanese CA *Ashigara* south of Java 1 Mar 42.
220	*MacLeish*	2 Aug 20	8 Mar 46	Reclassified AG-87 5 Jan 45. Stricken 13 Nov 46, sold, scrapped.
221	*Simpson*	3 Nov 20	29 May 46	Reclassified AG-97 23 May 45. Stricken 19 Jun 46, sold, scrapped.

Before the recommissionings began in 1929 at San Diego. Rust and red lead show through the gray on the Gillis. This ship was not among those tapped to rejoin the active fleet, and she was to await the passing of another decade before hoisting her pennant, as AVD-12. Photograph by Lieutenant Commander Don P. Moon.

Recommissioning of the Bernadou (DD-153) at Philadelphia, 1 May 1930, after eight years in reserve. She served with the Scouting Force until 1936, spent three more years in inactivity at Philadelphia, and broke her pennant again in October 1939. From then until decommissioned finally in July 1945, she served in the North Atlantic, Mediterranean, and Caribbean, earning a Presidential Unit Citation for her part in the invasion of French North Africa in November 1942. Photograph by courtesy of Captain Milton S. Davis.

No.	Name	1st Comm.	Decomm.	Disposition
222	*Bulmer*	16 Aug 20	16 Aug 46	Reclassified AG-86 30 Nov 44. Stricken 25 Sep 46, sold, scrapped.
223	*McCormick*	30 Aug 20	4 Oct 45	Reclassified AG-118 30 Jun 45. Stricken 24 Oct 45, sold, scrapped.
224	*Stewart*	15 Sep 20	2 Mar 42	Damaged, scuttled in dry dock at Soerabaja, Java, 2 Mar 42. Salved by Japanese Apr 43 and commissioned in Japanese Navy.
	P-102 (HIJMS)	15 Jun 43	5 Oct 45	Surrendered to US at Kure, Japan, 15 Oct 45.
	DD-224	29 Oct 45	23 May 46	Stricken, sunk as target by US aircraft off San Francisco 24 May 46.
225	*Pope*	27 Oct 20	1 Mar 42	Sunk by Japanese cruisers and aircraft in Java Sea 1 Mar 42.
226	*Peary*	22 Oct 20	19 Feb 42	Sunk by Japanese aircraft at Darwin, Australia, 19 Feb 42.
227	*Pillsbury*	15 Dec 20	1 Mar 42	Sunk by Japanese cruiser gunfire in Bali Strait, 1 Mar 42.
228	*Ford*	30 Dec 20		Renamed *John D. Ford* 17 Nov 21.
	John D. Ford		2 Nov 45	Reclassified AG-119 30 Jun 45. Stricken 16 Nov 45, sold, scrapped.
229	*Truxtun*	16 Feb 21	18 Feb 42	Grounded Placentia Bay, Newfoundland, 18 Feb 42, total loss.
230	*Paul Jones*	19 Apr 21	5 Nov 45	Reclassified AG-120 30 Jun 45. Stricken 28 Nov 45, sold, scrapped.
231	*Hatfield*	16 Apr 20	13 Dec 46	Reclassified AG-84 1 Oct 44. Stricken 28 Jan 47, sold, scrapped.
232	*Brooks*	18 Jun 20	2 Aug 45	Reclassified APD-10 31 Oct 42. Damaged by Japanese suicide aircraft at Lingayen Gulf 6 Jan 45, beyond repair. Stricken 17 Sep 45, sold, scrapped.
233	*Gilmer*	30 Apr 20	5 Feb 46	Reclassified APD-11 31 Oct 42. Stricken 25 Feb 46, sold, scrapped.
234	*Fox*	17 May 20	29 Nov 45	Reclassified AG-85 1 Oct 44. Stricken 19 Dec 45, sold, scrapped.
235	*Kane*	11 Jun 20	24 Jan 46	Reclassified APD-18 2 Jan 43. Stricken 25 Feb 45, sold, scrapped.
236	*Humphreys*	21 Jul 20	26 Oct 45	Reclassified APD-12 31 Oct 42. Reclassified DD-236 20 Jul 45. Stricken 13 Nov 45, sold, scrapped.
237	*McFarland*	30 Sep 20	8 Nov 45	Reclassified AVD-14 2 Aug 40. Reclassified DD-237 1 Dec 43. Stricken 19 Dec 45, sold, scrapped.
238	*James K. Paulding*	29 Nov 20	10 Feb 31	Stricken 25 Jan 37, hulk.
239	*Overton*	30 Jun 20	28 Jul 45	Reclassified APD-23 21 Aug 43. Stricken 13 Aug 45, sold, scrapped.
240	*Sturtevant*	21 Sep 20	26 Apr 42	Sunk in US minefield off Key West 26 Apr 42.
241	*Childs*	22 Oct 20	10 Dec 45	Reclassified AVP-14 1 Jul 38. Reclassified AVD-1 2 Aug 40. Stricken 3 Jan 46, sold, scrapped.
242	*King*	16 Dec 20	23 Oct 45	Stricken 16 Nov 45, sold, scrapped.
243	*Sands*	10 Nov 20	19 Oct 45	Reclassified APD-13 31 Oct 42. Stricken 1 Nov 45, sold, scrapped.
244	*Williamson*	29 Oct 20	8 Nov 45	Reclassified AVP-15 1 Jul 38. Reclassified AVD-2 2 Aug 40. Reclassified DD-244 1 Dec 43. Stricken 19 Dec 45, sold, scrapped.
245	*Reuben James*	24 Sep 20	31 Oct 41	Reclassified AVP-16 1 Aug 39. Designation cancelled 1 Oct 39. Sunk by German submarine U-562 while escorting a convoy in mid-Atlantic 31 Oct 41.
246	*Bainbridge*	9 Feb 21	21 Jul 45	Stricken 13 Aug 45, sold, scrapped.
247	*Goff*	19 Jan 21	21 Jul 45	Stricken 13 Aug 45, sold, scrapped.
248	*Barry*	28 Dec 20	21 Jun 45	Reclassified APD-29 15 Jan 44. Damaged beyond repair by Japanese suicide aircraft at Okinawa 25 May 45. Decommissioned 21 Jun 45 and sunk same day by suicide aircraft while under tow.

Forecastle of the John D. Ford (DD-228) while she was engaged against Chinese Communists in the Yangtze River, 18 September 1927. Officers are in blues; men in white hats and dungarees. A Lewis machine gun is just forward of the starboard billboard. Photograph by Lieutenant R. B. Tuggle.

No.	Name	1st Comm.	Decomm.	Disposition
249	Hopkins	21 Mar 21	21 Dec 45	Reclassified DMS-13 19 Nov 40. Stricken 8 Jan 46, sold, scrapped.
250	Lawrence	18 Apr 21	24 Oct 45	Stricken 13 Nov 45, sold, scrapped.
251	Belknap	28 Apr 19	4 Aug 45	Reclassified AVD-8 2 Aug 40. Reclassified DD-251 14 Nov 43. Reclassified APD-34 22 Jun 44. Damaged beyond repair by Japanese suicide aircraft at Lingayen Gulf 11 Jan 45. Stricken 13 Aug 45, sold, scrapped.
252	McCook	30 Apr 19	24 Sep 40	Transferred to UK 24 Sep 40.
	HMCS St. Croix	24 Sep 40	20 Sep 43	Sunk by German submarine in North Atlantic 20 Sep 43.
253	McCalla	19 May 19	23 Oct 40	Transferred to UK 23 Oct 40.
	HMS Stanley	23 Oct 40	19 Dec 41	Converted to convoy escort Jan 41. Sunk by German submarine U-574 west of Lisbon 19 Dec 41.
254	Rodgers (ex-Kalk)	22 Jul 19	23 Oct 40	Renamed 23 Dec 18. Transferred to UK 23 Oct 40.
	HMS Sherwood	23 Oct 40	26 May 43	Assigned as aircraft training ship Aug 42. Paid off 26 May 43 and used for spare parts. Hulk beached as aircraft target 30 Nov 43. Broken up 45.
255	Ingram	28 Jun 19		Renamed Osmond Ingram 11 Nov 19.
	Osmond Ingram		8 Jan 46	Reclassified AVD-9 2 Aug 40. Reclassified DD-255 4 Nov 43. Reclassified APD-35 22 Jun 44. Stricken 21 Jan 46, sold, scrapped.
256	Bancroft	30 Jun 19	24 Sep 40	Transferred to UK 24 Sep 40.
	HMCS St. Francis	24 Sep 40		Assigned as training tender 44. Declared surplus 1 Apr 45. Sold for scrap. Sunk in collision with SS Winding Gulf off Sagonnett Point, R. I., 14 Jul 45 while under tow.
257	Welles	2 Sep 19	9 Sep 40	Transferred to UK 9 Sep 40.
	HMS Cameron	9 Sep 40	5 Oct 43	Bombed and capsized in dry dock at Portsmouth, England, 5 Dec 40. Salved, used as hulk for shock tests. Paid off 5 Oct 43. Broken up Nov 44.
258	Aulick	26 Jul 19	8 Oct 40	Transferred to UK 8 Oct 40.
	HMS Burnham	8 Oct 40	Nov 44	Assigned as aircraft training ship Nov 43. Placed in reserve 1 Dec 44. Broken up 48.
259	Turner	24 Sep 19	7 Jun 22	Stricken 5 Aug 36. Converted to water barge and reclassified YW-56 23 Oct 36.
	YW-56	23 Oct 36	13 Feb 43	Converted to CIC training ship renamed Moosehead (IX-98) 13 Feb 43.
	Moosehead	13 Feb 43	19 Mar 46	Stricken 17 Apr 46. Disposed of through Maritime Commission 20 Feb 47. Scrapped.
260	Gillis	3 Sep 19	15 Oct 45	Reclassified AVD-12 2 Aug 40. Stricken 1 Nov 45, scrapped.
261	Delphy	30 Nov 18	8 Sep 23	Grounded Point Arguello, Calif., 8 Sep 23, total loss. Wreckage sold 19 Oct 25.
262	McDermut	27 Mar 19	22 May 29	Stricken 11 Nov 31, scrapped, sold.
263	Laub	17 Mar 19	8 Oct 40	Transferred to UK 8 Oct 40.
	HMS Burwell	8 Oct 40	Jan 45	Assigned as aircraft training ship Oct 43. Placed in reserve 29 Jan 45. Broken up 47.
264	McLanahan	5 Apr 19	8 Oct 40	Transferred to UK 8 Oct 40.
	HMS Bradford	8 Oct 40		Paid off as DD and recommissioned as accommodation ship 2 Jun 43. Disposed of for scrapping 46.
265	Edwards	24 Apr 19	8 Oct 40	Transferred to UK 8 Oct 40.
	HMS Buxton	8 Oct 40	2 Jun 45	Paid off as DD 4 Nov 43 and loaned to RCN as training tender. Paid off 2 Jun 45 in Canada. Sold and towed to US for scrapping Jun 45.
266	Greene (ex-Anthony)	9 May 19	24 Nov 45	Renamed 1 Aug 18. Reclassified AVD-13 2 Aug 40. Reclassified DD-266 4 Nov 43. Reclassified APD-36 1 Feb 44. Grounded in typhoon at Okinawa 9 Oct 45, total loss. Stricken 5 Dec 45.

Picture on pages 80 and 81 shows a flush decker and a Martin T4M torpedo plane launching torpedoes in 1930. The airplane, which could carry a single 18-inch weapon, was not yet a competitor to the destroyer, which could launch a dozen 21-inch torpedoes. But in World War II, airplanes were to launch many more torpedoes than destroyers did.

A Chinese junk sails past the stern of the Paul Jones (DD-230) anchored off Chefoo, China. For many years before World War II, a squadron of thirteen flush deckers, with the Paul Jones as flagship, served on the Asiatic station.

No.	Name	1st Comm.	Decomm.	Disposition
267	Ballard	5 Jun 19	5 Dec 45	Reclassified AVD-10 2 Aug 40. Stricken 3 Jan 46, sold, scrapped.
268	Shubrick	3 Jul 19	26 Nov 40	Transferred to UK 26 Nov 40.
	HMS Ripley	26 Nov 40	Jan 44	Placed in reserve 23 Feb 44. Broken up 45.
269	Bailey	27 Jun 19	26 Nov 40	Transferred to UK 26 Nov 40.
	HMS Reading	26 Nov 40		Assigned as aircraft training ship Oct 42. Placed in reserve 16 Jul 45. Broken up 45.
270	Thornton	15 Jul 19	2 May 45	Reclassified AVD-11 2 Aug 40. Damaged in collision with USS Ashtabula 5 Apr 45 and beached at Okinawa, total loss. Stricken 13 Aug 45.
271	Morris	21 Jul 19	15 Jun 22	Stricken 19 May 36, sold, hulk.
272	Tingey	25 Jul 19	24 May 22	Stricken 19 May 36, sold, hulk.
273	Swasey	8 Aug 19	26 Nov 40	Transferred to UK 26 Nov 40.
	HMS Rockingham	26 Nov 40	27 Sep 44	Assigned as aircraft training ship Dec 43. Sunk by mine off Aberdeen, Scotland, 27 Sep 44.
274	Meade	8 Sep 19	26 Nov 40	Transferred to UK 26 Nov 40.
	HMS Ramsey	26 Nov 40	30 Jun 45	Assigned as aircraft training ship Jun 43. Paid off and placed in reserve 30 Jun 45. Broken up 47.
275	Sinclair	8 Oct 19	1 Jun 30	Designated "Light Target #3" (IX-37) 5 Nov 30. Name and classification restored 11 Aug 31. Stricken 5 Jun 35, sold, scrapped.
276	McCawley	22 Sep 19	1 Apr 30	Stricken 13 Aug 30, scrapped, sold.
277	Moody	10 Dec 19	2 Jun 30	Stricken 3 Nov 30, sold. Sunk by purchaser 21 Feb 33 in motion picture.
278	Henshaw	10 Dec 19	11 Mar 30	Stricken 22 Jul 30, scrapped, sold.
279	Meyer	17 Dec 19	15 May 29	Stricken 25 Nov 30, scrapped, sold.
280	Doyen	17 Dec 19	25 Feb 30	Stricken 12 Jul 30, scrapped, sold.
281	Sharkey	28 Nov 19	1 May 30	Stricken 22 Oct 30, sold, scrapped.
282	Toucey	9 Dec 19	1 May 30	Stricken 22 Oct 30, sold, scrapped.
283	Breck	1 Dec 19	1 May 30	Stricken 22 Oct 30, sold, scrapped.
284	Isherwood	4 Dec 19	1 May 30	Stricken 22 Oct 30, sold, scrapped.
285	Case	8 Dec 19	1 May 30	Stricken 22 Oct 30, sold, scrapped.
286	Lardner	10 Dec 19	1 May 30	Stricken 22 Oct 30, sold, scrapped.
287	Putnam	18 Dec 19	1 May 30	Stricken 22 Oct 30, sold, hulk. Converted to merchant ship 31.
	MV Teapa			Banana carrier 31-42. U.S. Army freighter and training ship 42-45. Banana carrier 47-51. Sold for scrap May 55.
288	Worden	24 Feb 20	1 May 30	Stricken 22 Oct 30, sold, hulk. Converted to merchant ship 31.
	MV Tabasco			Banana carrier. Lost by grounding on Alacran Reef, Gulf of Mexico, 33.
289	Flusser	25 Feb 20	1 May 30	Stricken 22 Oct 30, sold, scrapped.
290	Dale	16 Feb 20	1 May 30	Stricken 22 Oct 30, sold, hulk. Converted to merchant ship.
	MV Masaya			Banana carrier 31-42. US Army freighter 42-43. Sunk by Japanese aircraft at Oro Bay, New Guinea, 28 Mar 43.
291	Converse	28 Apr 20	1 May 30	Stricken 22 Oct 30, sold, scrapped.
292	Reid	3 Dec 19	1 May 30	Stricken 22 Oct 30, sold, scrapped.
293	Billingsley	1 Mar 20	1 May 30	Stricken 22 Oct 30, sold, scrapped.
294	Charles Ausburn (ex-Ausburne)	23 Mar 20	1 May 30	Renamed 20 Feb 20. Stricken 22 Oct 30, sold, scrapped.
295	Osborne	17 May 20	1 May 30	Stricken 22 Oct 30, sold, hulk. Converted to merchant ship 31.
	MV Matagalpa			Banana carrier 31-42. US Army freighter 42. Burned at Sydney, Australia, 27 Jun 42 and scrapped.

A nest of four stackers at San Diego getting up steam for a cruise to Alaska with Naval Reservists in 1930. The nearest ship is the Twiggs, which, in 1940, became HMS Leamington and in 1944, the Russian Navy ship Zhguchi. Under the hammer and sickle she lasted until 1950. When this photograph was taken, a destroyer division consisted of six ships. Shortly after, this was changed to four ships each.

The Wasmuth (DD-338) in the floating dry dock ARD-1 at the San Diego Destroyer Base in June 1935. The dry dock flies both a jack and a commission pennant. Massive chains hold the dry dock in place. When this picture was taken, she was drawing almost 26 feet.

No.	Name	1st Comm.	Decomm.	Disposition
296	Chauncey	25 Jun 19	8 Sep 23	Grounded Point Arguello, Calif., 8 Sep 23, total loss. Wreckage sold 19 Oct 25.
297	Fuller	28 Feb 20	8 Sep 23	Grounded Point Arguello, Calif., 8 Sep 23, total loss. Wreckage sold 19 Oct 25.
298	Percival	21 Mar 20	6 Apr 30	Stricken 18 Nov 30, scrapped, sold.
299	John Francis Burnes (ex-Swasey)	1 May 20	25 Feb 30	Renamed 18 Oct 18. Stricken 22 Jul 30, scrapped, sold.
300	Farragut	4 Jun 20	1 Apr 30	Stricken 22 Jul 30, scrapped, sold.
301	Somers	23 Jun 20	10 Apr 30	Stricken 18 Nov 30, scrapped, sold.
302	Stoddert	30 Jun 20	10 Jan 33	Designated "Light Target #1" (IX-35) 5 Nov 30. Name and classification restored 24 Apr 31. Reclassified AG-18 30 Jun 31. Reclassified DD-302 16 Apr 32. Stricken 5 Jun 35, sold, scrapped.
303	Reno	23 Jul 20	18 Jan 30	Stricken 8 Jul 30, scrapped, sold.
304	Farquhar	5 Aug 20	20 Feb 30	Stricken 18 Nov 30, used as barracks ship, scrapped and sold 31.
305	Thompson	16 Aug 20	4 Apr 30	Stricken 22 Jul 30, scrapped, sold.
306	Kennedy	28 Aug 20	1 May 30	Stricken 18 Nov 30, scrapped, sold.
307	Paul Hamilton (ex-Hamilton)	24 Sep 20	20 Jan 30	Renamed 1 Apr 17. Stricken 8 Jul 30, scrapped, sold.
308	William Jones	30 Sep 20	24 May 30	Stricken 13 Aug 30, scrapped, sold.
309	Woodbury	20 Oct 20	8 Sep 23	Grounded Point Arguello, Calif., 8 Sept 23, total loss. Wreckage sold 19 Oct 25.
310	S. P. Lee (ex-Branch)	30 Oct 20	8 Sep 23	Renamed 12 May 19. Grounded Point Arguello, Calif., 8 Sep 23, total loss. Wreckage sold 19 Oct 25.
311	Nicholas	23 Nov 20	8 Sep 23	Grounded Point Arguello, Calif., 8 Sep 23, total loss. Wreckage sold 19 Oct 25.
312	Young	29 Nov 20	8 Sep 23	Grounded Point Arguello, Calif., 8 Sep 23, total loss. Wreckage sold 19 Oct 25.
313	Zeilin	10 Dec 20	22 Jan 30	Stricken 8 Jul 30, scrapped, sold.
314	Yarborough	31 Dec 20	29 May 30	Stricken 3 Nov 30, scrapped, sold.
315	La Vallette	24 Dec 20	19 Apr 30	Stricken 22 Jul 30, scrapped, sold.
316	Sloat	30 Dec 20	2 Jun 30	Stricken 28 Jan 35, sunk as gunfire target 26 Jun 35 off San Diego.
317	Wood	28 Jan 21	31 Mar 30	Stricken 22 Jul 30, scrapped, sold.
318	Shirk	5 Feb 21	8 Feb 30	Stricken 22 Jul 30, used as damage control hulk, scrapped, sold.
319	Kidder	7 Feb 21	18 Mar 30	Stricken 22 Jul 30, scrapped, sold.
320	Selfridge	17 Feb 21	8 Feb 30	Stricken 3 Nov 30, scrapped, sold.
321	Marcus	23 Feb 21	31 May 30	Stricken 28 Jan 35, sunk as gunfire target 25 Jun 35 off San Diego.
322	Mervine	1 Mar 21	4 Jun 30	Stricken 3 Nov 30, scrapped, sold.
323	Chase	10 Mar 21	15 May 30	Stricken 13 Aug 30, scrapped, sold.
324	Robert Smith	17 Mar 21	1 Mar 30	Stricken 12 Jul 30, scrapped, sold.
325	Mullany	29 Mar 21	1 May 30	Stricken 18 Nov 30, scrapped, sold.
326	Coghlan	31 Mar 21	1 May 30	Stricken 22 Oct 30, sold, scrapped.
327	Preston	13 Apr 21	1 May 30	Used for strength test, stricken 6 Nov 31, scrapped, sold.
328	Lamson	19 Apr 21	1 May 30	Stricken 22 Oct 30, sold, scrapped.
329	Bruce	29 Sep 20	1 May 30	Used for strength test, stricken 6 Nov 31, scrapped, sold.
330	Hull	26 Apr 21	31 Mar 30	Stricken 22 Jul 30, scrapped, sold.
331	MacDonough	30 Apr 21	8 Jan 30	Stricken 8 Jul 30, scrapped, sold.
332	Farenholt	10 May 21	20 Feb 30	Stricken 12 Jul 30, scrapped, sold.
333	Sumner	27 May 21	29 Mar 30	Stricken 18 Nov 30, used as barracks ship, scrapped and sold 34.
334	Corry	25 May 21	5 Feb 30	Stricken 22 Oct 30, sold, scrapped. Vallejo, Calif.
335	Melvin	31 May 21	8 May 30	Stricken 3 Nov 30, scrapped, sold.

The Ramsay (DM-16), still bearing her DD hull number, takes station in the screen around the battleship Arizona during Fleet maneuvers in the Pacific in 1936. Mine tracks run to the stern from abreast the aftermost funnels. The minelayers could perform all destroyer missions except torpedo attack.

A division of destroyers bursts through its own smoke during exercises carried out between the wars. Smoke could be used to shield one's own forces from a more powerful enemy or to provide a screen behind which one could organize a torpedo attack, and was to be used for both purposes by U.S. destroyers in World War II.

No.	Name	1st Comm.	Decomm.	Disposition
336	*Litchfield*	12 May 20	5 Nov 45	Reclassified AG-95 31 Mar 45. Stricken 28 Nov 45, scrapped.
337	*Zane*	15 Feb 21	15 Dec 45	Reclassified DMS-14 19 Nov 40. Reclassified AG-109 5 Jun 45. Stricken 8 Jan 46, sold, scrapped.
338	*Wasmuth*	16 Dec 21	29 Dec 42	Reclassified DMS-15 19 Nov 40. Foundered in storm off Aleutians 29 Dec 42.
339	*Trever*	3 Aug 22	23 Nov 45	Reclassified DMS-16 19 Nov 40. Reclassified AG-110 5 Jun 45. Stricken 5 Dec 45, sold, scrapped.
340	*Perry*	7 Aug 22	13 Sep 44	Reclassified DMS-17 19 Nov 40. Sunk by mine off Palau 13 Sep 44.
341	*Decatur*	9 Aug 22	28 Jul 45	Stricken 13 Aug 45, sold, scrapped.
342	*Hulbert*	27 Oct 20	2 Nov 45	Damaged in collision, repaired with bow from *Graham* (DD-192) 22. Reclassified AVP-19 15 Nov 39. Reclassified AVD-6 2 Aug 40. Reclassified DD-342 1 Dec 43. Stricken 28 Nov 45, sold, scrapped.
343	*Noa*	15 Feb 21	12 Sep 44	Reclassified APD-24 10 Aug 43. Sunk in collision with USS *Fullam* (DD-474) off Palau 12 Sep 44.
344	*William B. Preston*	23 Aug 20	6 Dec 45	Reclassified AVP-20 15 Nov 39. Reclassified AVD-7 2 Aug 40. Stricken 3 Jan 46, sold, scrapped.
345	*Preble*	19 Mar 20	7 Dec 45	Reclassified DM-20 30 Jun 37. Reclassified AG-99 5 Jun 45. Stricken 3 Jan 46, sold, scrapped.
346	*Sicard*	9 Jun 20	21 Nov 45	Reclassified DM-21 30 Jun 37. Reclassified AG-100 5 Jun 45. Stricken 19 Dec 45, sold, scrapped.
347	*Pruitt*	2 Sep 20	16 Nov 45	Reclassified DM-22 30 Jun 37. Reclassified AG-101 5 Jun 45. Stricken 5 Dec 45, scrapped.

Four-pipers on maneuvers in Alaskan waters in 1937. Spray is flung across the forecastle of the Long (DD-209) soon after she executed a turn to port that put the sea on her beam. She carries an impressive number of stays and shrouds to support her masts. Just as had many of her sisters, she has a set of spreaders below the crow's nest to provide a better angle for the upper shrouds.

Flush-Deck Destroyers Converted to DM (Light Minelayer or Destroyer Minelayer)

DM No.	Name	Former DD No.	DM No.	Name	Former DD No.
1	*Stribling*	96	12	*Anthony*	172
2	*Murray*	97	13	*Sproston*	173
3	*Israel*	98	14	*Rizal*	174
4	*Luce*	99	15	*Gamble*	123
5	*Maury*	100	16	*Ramsay*	124
6	*Lansdale*	101	17	*Montgomery*	121
7	*Mahan*	102	18	*Breese*	122
8	*Hart*	110	19	*Tracy*	214
9	*Ingraham*	111	20	*Preble*	345
10	*Ludlow*	112	21	*Sicard*	346
11	*Burns*	171	22	*Pruitt*	347

Flush-Deck Destroyers Converted to Seaplane Tenders (AVD, formerly AVP)

AVP No.	AVD No.	Name	Former DD No.	AVP No.	AVD No.	Name	Former DD No.
14	1	*Childs*	241	—	8	*Belknap*	251
15	2	*Williamson*	244	—	9	*Osmond Ingram*	255
16*	3	*George E. Badger*	196	—	10	*Ballard*	267
17	4	*Clemson*	186	—	11	*Thornton*	270
18	5	*Goldsborough*	188	—	12	*Gillis*	260
19	6	*Hulbert*	342	—	13	*Greene*	266
20	7	*William B. Preston*	344	—	14	*McFarland*	237

* Reuben James (DD-245) was originally designated AVP-16, but the designation was canceled and George E. Badger substituted.

Flush-Deck Destroyers Converted to High-Speed Minesweepers (DMS)

DMS No.	Name	Former DD No.	DMS No.	Name	Former DD No.
1	Dorsey	117	10	Southard	207
2	Lamberton	119	11	Hovey	208
3	Boggs	136	12	Long	209
4	Elliot	146	13	Hopkins	249
5	Palmer	161	14	Zane	337
6	Hogan	178	15	Wasmuth	338
7	Howard	179	16	Trever	339
8	Stansbury	180	17	Perry	340
9	Chandler	206	18	Hamilton	141

Flush-Deck Destroyers Converted to High-Speed Transports (APD)

APD No.	Name	Former DD No.	APD No.	Name	Former DD No.
1	Manley	74	17	Crosby	164
2	Colhoun	85	18	Kane	235
3	Gregory	82	19	Tattnall	125
4	Little	79	20	Roper	147
5	McKean	90	21	Dickerson	157
6	Stringham	83	22	Herbert	160
7	Talbot	114	23	Overton	239
8	Waters	115	24	Noa	343
9	Dent	116	25	Rathburne	113
10	Brooks	232	29	Barry	248
11	Gilmer	233	31	Clemson	186
12	Humphreys	236	32	Goldsborough	188
13	Sands	243	33	George E. Badger	196
14	Schley	103	34	Belknap	251
15	Kilty	137	35	Osmond Ingram	255
16	Ward	139	36	Greene	266

Note: Hull numbers APD-26 through 28 were reserved for *McFarland* (DD-237), *Williamson* (DD-244), and *Hulbert* (DD-342) respectively, but the ships were never officially reclassified or converted to APDs. There never was an APD-30.

Flush-Deck Destroyers Converted to Miscellaneous Auxiliary (AG)

AG No.	Name	Former DD No.	AG No.	Name	Former DD No.
18	Stoddert	302	100	Sicard	346
19	Boggs	136	101	Pruitt	347
20	Kilty	137	102	Babbitt	128
21	Lamberton	119	103	Upshur	144
22*	Radford	120	104	Eliot	146
24	Semmes	189	105	Hogan	178
28	Manley	74	106	Howard	179
80	Dupont	152	107	Stansbury	180
81	J. Fred Talbott	156	108	Chandler	206
82	Schenck	159	109	Zane	337
83	Kennison	138	110	Trever	339
84	Hatfield	231	111	Hamilton	141
85	Fox	234	112	Breckinridge	148
86	Bulmer	222	113	Barney	149
87	MacLeish	220	114	Biddle	151
91	Dahlgren	187	115	Ellis	154
95	Litchfield	336	116	Cole	155
96	Broome	210	117	Whipple	217
97	Simpson	221	118	McCormick	223
98	Ramsey	124	119	John D. Ford	228
99	Preble	345	120	Paul Jones	230

* Designation canceled, destroyer classification restored.

Pages 90 and 91. The aircraft carrier Saratoga comes under the protection of a division of four-pipers during maneuvers in 1929. The nearest destroyer is the Preble (DD-345), next the Hulbert (DD-342), and third the Pruitt (DD-347). This was the year when the Saratoga demonstrated the potential of the carrier task force, off the coast of Central America.

First hit of World War II. These men of the USS Ward (DD-139) stand by the 4-inch gun with which they fired on and hit a Japanese midget submarine surfaced near the entrance to Pearl Harbor at 0645 on 7 December 1941, more than an hour before the air attacks began. Their helmets are veterans of the same war as their ship.

Flush-Deck Destroyers Which Served with the Coast Guard

No.	Name	Dates	USCG No.
189	*Semmes*	4-25-32 to 4-20-34	20
193	*Abel P. Upshur*	11-5-30 to 5-21-34	15
194	*Hunt*	9-13-30 to 5-28-34	18
195	*Welborn C. Wood*	10-1-30 to 5-21-34	19
196	*George E. Badger*	10-1-30 to 5-21-34	16
198	*Herndon*	9-13-30 to 5-28-34	17

Flush-Deck Destroyers Redesignated Unclassified (IX)

IX Number and Name		DD Number and Name	
35	Light Target No. 1	302	*Stoddert*
36	Light Target No. 2	107	*Hazelwood* (canceled)
		136	*Boggs*
37	Light Target No. 3	275	*Sinclair* (canceled)
		137	*Kilty*
44	DCH-1	163	*Walker*
98	*Moosehead*	259	*Turner*

Flush-Deck Destroyers Converted to Water Barges (YW)

YW Number	DD Number and Name	
56	259	*Turner*
57	163	*Walker*

Some of the four stackers came to a spectacular end, as did the British Campbeltown, *seen just before she blew up after ramming the dock gate at St. Nazaire, France, on 28 March 1942. By so sacrificing this ship, the British ended any hopes the Germans might have had of using the only dry dock on the French Atlantic coast that could be used to repair the battleship* Tirpitz. *Photograph by courtesy of the Imperial War Museum.*

But the Canadian Columbia, *after she rammed a cliff, ended her days as a hulk at Liverpool, Nova Scotia, serving as a storage depot for fuel and ammunition removed from ships under overhaul. Official Canadian Navy photograph. The* Columbia *originally was the USS* Haraden (DD-183) *and the Campbeltown, USS* Buchanan (DD-131).

British "Town" Class Destroyers

Pendant No.	British Name	U.S. Name	Hull No.
I-04	*Annapolis* (RCN)	*Mackenzie*	175
I-17	*Bath*	*Hopewell*	181
H-46	*Belmont*	*Satterlee*	190
H-64	*Beverley*	*Branch*	197
H-72	*Bradford*	*McLanahan*	264
I-08	*Brighton*	*Cowell*	167
H-81	*Broadwater*	*Mason*	191
H-90	*Broadway*	*Hunt*	194
H-82	*Burnham*	*Aulick*	258
H-94	*Burwell*	*Laub*	263
H-96	*Buxton*	*Edwards*	265
I-20	*Caldwell*	*Hale*	133
I-05	*Cameron*	*Welles*	257
I-42	*Campbeltown*	*Buchanan*	131
I-23	*Castleton*	*Aaron Ward*	132
I-21	*Charlestown*	*Abbot*	184
I-35	*Chelsea*	*Crowninshield*	134
I-28	*Chesterfield*	*Welborn C. Wood*	195
I-45	*Churchill*	*Herndon*	198
I-14	*Clare*	*Abel P. Upshur*	193
I-49	*Columbia* (RCN)	*Haraden*	183
I-40	*Georgetown*	*Maddox*	168
I-24	*Hamilton* (RN, RCN)	*Kalk*	170
G-05	*Lancaster*	*Philip*	76
G-19	*Leamington*	*Twiggs*	127
G-27	*Leeds*	*Conner*	72
G-68	*Lewes*	*Conway*	70
G-42	*Lincoln*	*Yarnall*	143
G-57	*Ludlow*	*Stockton*	73
G-76	*Mansfield*	*Evans*	78
G-95	*Montgomery*	*Wickes*	75

TEMPORARY BOW

U. S. S. BLAKE
PHOTO #24
PHILA. NAVY

Pendant No.	British Name		U.S. Name	Hull No.
G-08	*Newark*		*Ringgold*	89
G-47	*Newmarket*		*Robinson*	88
G-54	*Newport*		*Sigourney*	81
I-57	*Niagara* (RCN)		*Thatcher*	162
G-60	*Ramsey*		*Meade*	274
G-71	*Reading*		*Bailey*	269
G-88	*Richmond*		*Fairfax*	93
G-79	*Ripley*		*Shubrick*	268
G-58	*Rockingham*		*Swasey*	273
I-07	*Roxborough*		*Foote*	169
I-15	*St. Albans*		*Thomas*	182
I-65	*St. Clair* (RCN)		*Williams*	108
I-81	*St. Croix* (RCN)		*McCook*	252
I-93	*St. Francis* (RCN)		*Bancroft*	256
I-12	*St. Marys*		*Doran*	185
I-52	*Salisbury*		*Claxton*	140
I-80	*Sherwood*		*Rodgers*	254
I-73	*Stanley*		*McCalla*	253
I-95	*Wells*		*Tillman*	135

Unit Citations and Commendations Awarded to Flush Deckers in World War II

Presidential Unit Citations

The Blakeley (DD-150), hit by a torpedo from a U-boat off Martinique in May 1942, lost her bow but survived. A temporary bow was fitted and the damaged destroyer steamed to Philadelphia, where the hulk of the stricken Taylor (DD-94) lay, overshadowed by an oiler at the other side of the pier. The ex-Taylor and Blakeley were dry-docked and the bow of the one was grafted onto the hull of the other. The Blakeley spent most of her war career in the Caribbean.

Barry (DD-248)	27 Jul-25 Oct 1943	As part of TU 21.14 (USS *Card* hunter/killer team)
Belknap (AVD-8)	20 Apr-20 Jun 1943	As part of TG 21.12 (USS *Bogue* hunter/killer team)
Bernadou (DD-153)	8 Nov 1942	Safi landings
Borie (DD-215)	27 Jul-25 Oct 1943	As part of TU 21.14 (USS *Card* hunter/killer team)
Clemson (AVD-4)	12 Jul-23 Aug 1943	As part of TG 21.13 (USS *Bogue* hunter/killer team)
Second Award	14 Nov-29 Dec 1943	As part of TG 21.13 (USS *Bogue* hunter/killer team)
Cole (DD-155)	8 Nov 1942	Safi landings
Dallas (DD-199)	10 Nov 1942	Port Lyautey landings
DuPont (DD-152)	14 Nov-29 Dec 1943	As part of TG 21.13 (USS *Bogue* hunter/killer team)
George E. Badger (AVD-3)	20 Apr-20 Jun 1943	As part of TG 21.12 (USS *Bogue* hunter/killer team)
Second Award	12 Jul-23 Aug 1943	As part of TG 21.13 (USS *Bogue* hunter/killer team)
Third Award	14 Nov-29 Dec 1943	As part of TG 21.13 (USS *Bogue* hunter/killer team)
Goff (DD-247)	27 Jul-25 Aug 1943	As part of TU 21.14 (USS *Bogue* hunter/killer team)
Greene (AVD-13)	20 Apr-20 Jun 1943	As part of TG 21.12 (USS *Bogue* hunter/killer team)
John D. Ford (DD-228)	23 Jan-2 Mar 1942	Java Sea operations
Lea (DD-118)	20 Apr-20 Jun 1943	As part of TG 21.12 (USS *Bogue* hunter/killer team)
McFarland (AVD-14)	20 Jun-16 Oct 1942	Southwest Pacific
Osmond Ingram (AVD-9)	20 Apr-20 Jun 1943	As part of TG 21.12 (USS *Bogue* hunter/killer team)
Second Award	12 Jul-23 Aug 1943	As part of TG 21.13 (USS *Bogue* hunter/killer team)
Third Award	14 Nov-29 Dec 1943	As part of TG 21.13 (USS *Bogue* hunter/killer team)
Pope (DD-225)	23 Jan-1 Mar 1942	Southwest Pacific

Navy Unit Commendations

Brooks (APD-10)	7 citations 4 Sep 43 - 6 Jan 45, Pacific
Crosby (APD-17)	7 citations 30 Jun 43 - 13 May 45, Pacific
Gilmer (APD-11)	7 citations 4 Sep 43 - 9 Apr 45, Pacific
Hamilton (DMS-18)	12-15 Sep 44 as part of TU 32.9.3 at Palau
Hopkins (DMS-13)	6-7 Jan 45, Lingayen
Second Commendation	7 Aug 42 - 4 Jun 44, Solomons
Hovey (DMS-11)	7 Aug 42 - 17 May 44, Solomons
Second Commendation	12-15 Sep 44 as part of TU 32.9.3 at Palau

Navy Unit Commendations (Continued)

Kilty (APD-15)	19 citations 2 May 43 - 7 May 45, Pacific
Long (DMS-12)	12-15 Sep 44 as part of TU 32.9.3 at Palau
Manley (APD-1)	13 citations 17 Aug 42 - 18 Feb 45, Pacific
McKean (APD-5)	3 citations 7 Aug 42 - 17 Nov 43, SW Pacific
Montgomery (DM-17)	12-15 Sep 44 as part of TU 32.9.3 at Palau
Sands (APD-13)	11 citations 29 Jan 43 - 14 Jun 45, Pacific
Southard (DMS-10)	7 Aug 42 - 17 May 44, SW Pacific
Stringham (APD-6)	9 citations 17 Aug 42 - 28 Apr 45, Pacific
Trever (DMS-16)	7 Aug 42 - 22 Jun 44, SW Pacific
Ward (APD-16)	8 citations 7 Dec 41 - 7 Dec 44, Pacific
Zane (DMS-14)	7 Aug 42 - 1 Aug 43, SW Pacific

Flush-Deck Destroyers—Cross Index of Names to Hull Numbers

The **Badger** *(DD-126) escorts a British oil tanker across the Atlantic. Some merchant tankers, such as this one, were fitted for limited fueling of warships at sea, and this was particularly useful for short-legged escorts, especially when any amount of high-speed steaming was necessary. The* **Badger's** *designed range of 4,500 nautical miles at 14 knots was increased during the war by the substitution of fuel tanks for her fourth boiler and stack.*

A night surface action in mid-Atlantic between the U-405 and the **Borie** *(DD-215) ended with the loss of both ships. After an hour's exchange of gunfire in 15-foot seas, the four-piper rammed the U-boat and action continued with small arms until the ships were wrenched apart by the waves. Using gunfire, torpedoes, and depth charges, the* **Borie** *finally overcame the foe, but was herself so damaged that she had to be abandoned. The hulk was sunk by our own carrier planes, one of which took this picture. To the end, she had her four stacks and 4-inch guns.*

132	Aaron Ward	299	Burnes, John Francis	341	Decatur
184	Abbot	258	Burnham (HMS)	129	Delong
193	Abel P. Upshur	171	Burns	261	Delphy
211	Alden	263	Burwell (HMS)	116	Dent
199	Alexander Dallas	166	Bush	157	Dickerson
175	Annapolis (HMCS)	265	Buxton (HMS)	169	Doblestny (USSR)
172	Anthony	69	Caldwell	185	Doran
266	Anthony (ex)	133	Caldwell (HMS)	117	Dorsey
258	Aulick	267	Cameron (HMS)	182	Dostoiny (USSR)
294	Ausburn, Charles	131	Campbeltown (HMS)	280	Doyen
128	Babbitt	285	Case	143	Druzhny (USSR)
126	Badger	132	Castleton (HMS)	152	Dupont
196	Badger, George E.	104	Champlin	84	Dyer
185	Bagley	206	Chandler	134	Dyerzki (USSR)
269	Bailey	294	Charles Ausburn	198	Dyeyatelny (USSR)
246	Bainbridge	184	Charlestown (HMS)	219	Edsall
267	Ballard	323	Chase	265	Edwards
256	Bancroft	296	Chauncey	216	Edwards, John D.
213	Barker	134	Chelsea (HMS)	146	Elliot
149	Barney	195	Chesterfield (HMS)	154	Ellis
248	Barry	106	Chew	78	Evans
181	Bath (HMS)	241	Childs	93	Fairfax
251	Belknap	198	Churchill (HMS)	332	Farenholt
95	Bell	193	Clare (HMS)	304	Farquhar
190	Belmont (HMS)	140	Claxton	300	Farragut
153	Bernadou	186	Clemson	289	Flusser
197	Beverly (HMS)	326	Coghlan	169	Foote
151	Biddle	155	Cole	228	Ford
293	Billingsley	85	Colhoun	228	Ford, John D.
150	Blakeley	183	Columbia (HMS)	234	Fox
136	Boggs	72	Conner	297	Fuller
215	Borie	291	Converse	123	Gamble
264	Bradford (HMS)	70	Conway	196	George E. Badger
197	Branch	334	Corry	168	Georgetown (HMS)
283	Breck	167	Cowell	260	Gillis
148	Breckinridge	139	Cowell (ex)	233	Gilmer
122	Breese	109	Crane	247	Goff
167	Brighton (HMS)	70	Craven	188	Goldsborough
191	Broadwater (HMS)	164	Crosby	192	Graham
194	Broadway (HMS)	134	Crowninshield	266	Greene
232	Brooks	187	Dahlgren	145	Greer
210	Broome	290	Dale	82	Gregory
329	Bruce	199	Dallas	92	Gridley
131	Buchanan	199	Dallas, Alexander	71	Gwin
222	Bulmer	163	DCH-1	133	Hale

141	*Hamilton*
307	*Hamilton (ex)*
170	*Hamilton (HMS) (HMCS)*
307	*Hamilton, Paul*
183	*Haraden*
91	*Harding*
110	*Hart*
231	*Hatfield*
107	*Hazelwood*
278	*Henshaw*
160	*Herbert*
198	*Herndon*
178	*Hogan*
181	*Hopewell*
249	*Hopkins*
208	*Hovey*
179	*Howard*
342	*Hulbert*
330	*Hull*
236	*Humphreys*
194	*Hunt*
111	*Ingraham*
255	*Ingram, Osmond*
284	*Isherwood*
98	*Israel*
130	*Jacob Jones*
238	*James K. Paulding*
245	*James, Reuben*
150	*J. Fred Talbott*
216	*John D. Edwards*
228	*John D. Ford*
299	*John Francis Burnes*
130	*Jones, Jacob*
230	*Jones, Paul*
308	*Jones, William*
170	*Kalk*
254	*Kalk (ex)*
235	*Kane*
306	*Kennedy*
138	*Kennison*
319	*Kidder*
137	*Kilty*
80	*Kimberly*
242	*King*
119	*Lamberton*
328	*Lamson*
76	*Lancaster (HMS)*
101	*Lansdale*
286	*Lardner*
263	*Laub*
315	*La Vallette*
250	*Lawrence*
118	*Lea*
127	*Leamington (HMS)*
158	*Leary*
310	*Lee, S. P.*
72	*Leeds (HMS)*
70	*Lewes (HMS)*
302	*Light Target No. 1*

136	*Light Target No. 2*
107	*Light Target No. 2 (ex)*
137	*Light Target No. 3*
275	*Light Target No. 3 (ex)*
143	*Lincoln (HMS)*
336	*Litchfield*
79	*Little*
209	*Long*
99	*Luce*
112	*Ludlow*
73	*Ludlow (HMS)*
331	*Macdonough*
175	*Mackenzie*
220	*MacLeish*
168	*Maddox*
102	*Mahan*
74	*Manley*
78	*Mansfield (HMS)*
321	*Marcus*
290	*Masaya (MV)*
191	*Mason*
295	*Matagalpa (MV)*
100	*Maury*
253	*McCalla*
276	*McCawley*
252	*McCook*
223	*McCormick*
262	*McDermut*
237	*McFarland*
90	*McKean*
87	*McKee*
264	*McLanahan*
274	*Meade*
335	*Melvin*
165	*Meredith*
322	*Mervine*
279	*Meyer*
121	*Montgomery*
75	*Montgomery (HMS)*
277	*Moody*
259	*Moosehead*
271	*Morris*
105	*Mugford*
325	*Mullany*
97	*Murray*
89	*Newark (HMS)*
88	*Newmarket (HMS)*
81	*Newport (HMS)*
162	*Niagara (HMCS)*
311	*Nicholas*
343	*Noa*
177	*O'Bannon*
295	*Osborne*
255	*Osmond Ingram*
239	*Overton*
161	*Palmer*
218	*Parrott*
238	*Paulding, James K.*
307	*Paul Hamilton*

230	*Paul Jones*
226	*Peary*
298	*Percival*
340	*Perry*
76	*Philip*
227	*Pillsbury*
225	*Pope*
345	*Preble*
327	*Preston*
344	*Preston, William B.*
347	*Pruitt*
287	*Putnam*
224	*P-102 (HIJMS)*
120	*Radford*
124	*Ramsay*
274	*Ramsey (HMS)*
113	*Rathburne*
269	*Reading (HMS)*
292	*Reid*
303	*Reno*
176	*Renshaw*
245	*Reuben James*
93	*Richmond (HMS)*
89	*Ringgold*
268	*Ripley (HMS)*
174	*Rizal*
324	*Robert Smith*
88	*Robinson*
273	*Rockingham (HMS)*
254	*Rodgers*
170	*Rodgers (ex)*
147	*Roper*
169	*Roxborough (HMS)*
182	*St. Albans (HMS)*
108	*St. Clair (HMCS)*
252	*St. Croix (HMCS)*
256	*St. Francis (HMCS)*
185	*St. Marys (HMS)*
140	*Salisbury (HMS)*
243	*Sands*
190	*Satterlee*
159	*Schenck*
103	*Schley*
99	*Schley (ex)*
320	*Selfridge*
189	*Semmes*
281	*Sharkey*
254	*Sherwood (HMS)*
318	*Shirk*
268	*Shubrick*
346	*Sicard*
81	*Sigourney*
221	*Simpson*
275	*Sinclair*
316	*Sloat*
324	*Smith, Robert*
212	*Smith Thompson*
301	*Somers*
207	*Southard*

Pages 100 and 101. The four-pipers continued with the Fleet right up to the end of the war. Here, one of them, converted to a DMS, joins a Fletcher-class destroyer in screening a battleship and three heavy cruisers steaming west toward Japanese-occupied Guam in 1944.

Top picture, opposite, shows a chief torpedoman's mate inspecting depth charges in their racks on the fantail of a flush decker at sea in the North Atlantic. The spray whips almost horizontally across the narrow deck. Lower picture, taken in the Pacific, shows the Moosehead (IX-98) taking oil from a heavy cruiser while both ships steam at over 25 knots. Moosehead's skipper believes this operation to have been the first high-speed refueling at sea. Photo by courtesy of Captain W. D. Acker.

Cross Index of Names to Hull Numbers (Continued)

310	*S. P. Lee*	305	*Thompson*	75	*Wickes*
173	*Sproston*	212	*Thompson, Smith*	344	*William B. Preston*
253	*Stanley* (HMS)	270	*Thornton*	308	*William Jones*
180	*Stansbury*	135	*Tillman*	108	*Williams*
86	*Stevens*	272	*Tingey*	244	*Williamson*
224	*Stewart*	282	*Toucey*	317	*Wood*
73	*Stockton*	214	*Tracy*	309	*Woodbury*
302	*Stoddert*	339	*Trever*	195	*Wood, Welborn C.*
96	*Stribling*	229	*Truxtun*	77	*Woolsey*
83	*Stringham*	259	*Turner*	288	*Worden*
240	*Sturtevant*	127	*Twiggs*	314	*Yarborough*
333	*Sumner*	144	*Upshur*	143	*Yarnall*
273	*Swasey*	193	*Upshur, Abel P.*	312	*Young*
288	*Tabasco* (MV)	163	*Walker*	259	*YW-56*
114	*Talbot*	139	*Ward*	163	*YW-57*
156	*Talbott, J. Fred*	132	*Ward, Aaron*	337	*Zane*
142	*Tarbell*	338	*Wasmuth*	313	*Zeilin*
125	*Tattnall*	115	*Waters*	167	*Zharki* (USSR)
94	*Taylor*	195	*Welborn C. Wood*	127	*Zhguchi* (USSR)
287	*Teapa* (MV)	257	*Welles*	93	*Zhivuchi* (USSR)
162	*Thatcher*	135	*Wells* (HMS)	168	*Zhyostki* (USSR)
182	*Thomas*	217	*Whipple*		

End of the Ward (APD-16). Three years and three hours after firing the first gun of the war in the Pacific, this little ship was struck by a kamikaze (0945, 7 December 1944). The suicide plane hit the port side just above the waterline and entered the boiler room. She lost all power and shortly had to be abandoned and sunk.

But most of the flush deckers ended their lives quietly. Here, five of them, decommissioned, lie at a temporary anchorage at Cape May, New Jersey, before being scrapped. The nearest is Blakeley (DD-150), wearing her number on the ex-Taylor's bow. Beyond two hulls which cannot be identified, are the John D. Edwards (DD-216) and Alexander Dallas (DD-199).

Cross Index of Russian Names to British and U.S. Names

Russian Name	British Name	U.S. Name	Number
Doblestny (Valiant)	*Roxborough*	*Foote*	169
Dostoiny (Worthy)	*St. Albans*	*Thomas*	182
Dyeyatelni (Active)	*Chelsea*	*Crowninshield*	134
Dyeyatelni (Active)	*Churchill*	*Herndon*	198
Druzhny (Friendly)	*Lincoln*	*Yarnall*	143
Zharki (Ardent)	*Brighton*	*Cowell*	167
Zhguchi (Fiery)	*Leamington*	*Twiggs*	127
Zhivuchi (Enduring)	*Richmond*	*Fairfax*	93
Zhyostki (Enterprising)	*Georgetown*	*Maddox*	168

Bibliography

Barker, F. V. "How the Navy Helped Them Home," *U.S. Naval Institute Proceedings*, Vol. 51 (August, 1925), pp. 1415-1445.

Bernhardt, John W., and Foster Hailey. "Saga of the Unsung—the Destroyer Transports," *USNIP*, Vol. 71 (February, 1945), pp. 177-185.

Chandler, T. E. "American and British Destroyers," *USNIP*, Vol. 48 (April, 1922), pp. 585-591.

Chaplin, Philip A. "The Reincarnation of the Four-Stackers," *USNIP*, Vol. 86 (March, 1960), pp. 95-99.

Fahey, James C. *Ships and Aircraft of the United States Fleet*. Falls Church, Virginia: Ships and Aircraft, (Seven editions from 1939-1958).

Field, Richard S. "A Destroyer in the Near East," *USNIP*, Vol. 51 (February, 1925), pp. 246-267; (March, 1925), pp. 400-423.

Glover, R. O. "Practical Hints on Handling a Destroyer," *USNIP*, Vol. 48 (January, 1922), pp. 57-67.

Great Britain. *The "Town" Class Destroyers*. (London: The Admiralty, 1949), p. 107.

Hadaway, Richard B. "Course Zero Nine Five," *USNIP*, Vol. 83 (January, 1957), pp. 40-48.

Hains, Paul W. "How the *Cushing* Towed in the *Murray*," *USNIP*, Vol. 46 (October, 1920), pp. 1619-1625.

Jane's Fighting Ships. New York & London: various publishers, 1917-1950.

Kell, C. O. "Investigation of Structural Characteristics of Destroyers *Preston* and *Bruce*," *Society of Naval Architects and Marine Engineers Transactions*, Vol. 39 (1931), pp. 35-62.

Kussart, Walter. "Reservicing Spotting Planes Underway During World War II," *USNIP*, Vol. 86 (October, 1960), pp. 107-109.

Lockwood, Charles A. and Hans C. Adamson. *Tragedy at Honda*. (Philadelphia: Chilton Co., 1960), p. 243.

Lott, Arnold S. *A Long Line of Ships*. (Annapolis: U.S. Naval Institute, 1954), p. 268.

Manning, T. D. *The British Destroyer*. (London: Putnam & Co., Ltd., 1961), p. 148.

Moon, D. P. "Recommissioning the Destroyers," *USNIP*, Vol. 57 (February, 1931), pp. 162-174.

Morison, Samuel Eliot. *History of United States Naval Operations in World War II*. (Boston: Little, Brown and Company, 1947-1961), 15 volumes.

Morton, Louis. *U.S. Army in World War II—The War in the Pacific—The Fall of the Philippines*. (Washington, D.C.: Government Printing Office, 1953), p. 626.

Nelson, William. "Salvage of the USS *De Long* (#129)," *USNIP*, Vol. 48 (September, 1922), pp. 1345-1363.

Owen, W. C. and J. F. Shafroth. "War-Time Destroyer Program," *Journal American Society of Naval Engineers*, Vol. 34 (August, 1922), pp. 345-384.

Phillips, C. E. Lucas. *The Greatest Raid of All*. (London: Heinemann & Co., 1958), p. 288.

Robinson, S. M. "The Evolution of the Destroyer," *JASNE*, Vol. 31 (November, 1919), pp. 900-910.

Roscoe, Theodore. *United States Destroyer Operations in World War II*. (Annapolis: U. S. Naval Institute, 1953), p. 581.

Rossell, H. E. "Types of Naval Ships," *SNAME Historical Transactions 1893-1943*. (New York: Society of Naval Architects and Marine Engineers, 1945), pp. 248-329.

Saunders, H. E. and A. S. Pitre. "Full Scale Trials on a Destroyer," *SNAME Transactions*, Vol. 41 (1933), pp. 243-295.

Taussig, J. K. "Destroyer Experiences during the Great War," *USNIP*, Vol. 48 (December, 1922), pp. 2015-2040; Vol. 49 (January, 1923), pp. 39-69; (February, 1923), pp. 221-248; (March, 1923), pp. 383-408.

Thomas, Donald I. "The Four Stackers," *USNIP*, Vol. 76 (July, 1950), pp. 753-757.

Thurber, H. R. "Some Notes on Destroyer Handling Alongside," *USNIP*, Vol. 51 (June, 1925), pp. 1203-1216.

Tilley, B. F. "Handling 117 Decommissioned Destroyers," *USNIP*, Vol. 49 (May, 1923), pp. 1105-1111.

U.S. Bureau of Construction and Repair and Bureau of Ships. *Ships' Data, U. S. Naval Vessels*. (Washington, D.C.: Government Printing Office, 1917-1948).

U.S. Naval History Division. *Dictionary of American Naval Fighting Ships*. Vol. I (A–B) and Vol II. (C–F). (Washington, D.C.: GPO, 1959).

U.S. Naval History Division. *United States Naval Chronology, World War II*. (Washington, D.C.: GPO, 1955), p. 214.

U.S. Naval History Division. Mimeographed ship's histories of various ships.

U.S. Navy Department. Annual Reports of the Secretary of the Navy, 1917-1932.

U.S. Navy Department. *U.S. Naval Aviation 1910-1960*. (NavWeps 00-80P-1). (Washington, D.C.: GPO, 1961).

Van Deurs, G. "A Commodore's Namesake," *USNIP*, Vol. 81 (June, 1955), pp. 678-684.

Weems, P. V. H. "Decommissioning Destroyers at Philadelphia," *USNIP*, Vol. 49 (February, 1923), pp. 449-452.

Williams, H. "A Record in Destroyer Construction," *USNIP*, Vol. 46 (March, 1920), pp. 531-538.

Information was also obtained from personal correspondence with individuals mentioned, and from many periodicals, too numerous to list, but including the following:

All Hands
Our Navy
The Illustrated London News

National Archives, and the records of the Department of the Navy's Bureau of Ships and Naval History Division were consulted.

Nine destroyers are reduced to scrap in the Philadelphia Navy Yard. One of them, the middle ship in the nearest row, is a flush decker. She displays a lonely steering wheel in what was her emergency steering station.

Addenda to the Reprinted Edition

Page 1: According to John C. Niedermair and others, Dr. James L. Bates of the Bureau of Construction and Repair had a large part in the design of the flush deckers.

Page 2: Philip A. C. Chaplin has identified the shapes on the after deckhouse of the *Schenck* (DD-159) as gear casings for the main engines.

Page 3: To clarify the text, the *Stockton* (DD-73) carried a total of five 4-inch/50 guns, two of which were in a twin mount.

Page 5: The inexperienced Filipino crew of the *Rizal* is reputed to have nearly wrecked the engines, necessitating the assignment of practically a duplicate U.S. crew.

Page 9: A former crew member of the *Hulbert* (DD-342), Andrew J. Stevens, has written that the ship's bow was damaged by ramming the *Hopkins* (DD-249). He also noted that the *Mason* (DD-191) rammed the *Satterlee* (DD-190) at about that time.

Page 11: C. A. Woolard, who served on the *Mugford* (DD-105), has recounted that his ship was the tender for the seaplanes *NC-5* and *NC-6*. During operations along the Pacific coast, the *NC-5* became disabled at La Union, Salvador. En route there, the *Mugford* burned out her boiler tubes and had to be towed into port. She was pulled out by the oiler *Kanawha* and turned over to an oceangoing tug, with the destroyer in turn towing the airplane. The rough waves proved too much for the *NC-5*, and her crew had to sink her with machine-gun fire. Later the *Mugford* had her screws removed at Balboa and was towed to Mare Island for repairs.

Page 12: The temporary deckhouse in the photo of the *Osborne* (DD-295), is reported to have held experimental gyro-stabilizing equipment.

Page 15: The hulk of the *Corry* (DD-334) lies in the east bank of the Napa River about three miles from Vallejo. (Also note in table on page 87.) Thomas J. Ryan has written that the hulk of another destroyer, possibly the *Kennedy* (DD-306), was still visible in 1965 in San Francisco Bay between the San Mateo and Dumbarton bridges.

Page 19: John J. Chester, a former chief engineer of the *Dahlgren* (ex-DD-187), has added that the flash-type high-pressure boilers were a constant source of trouble.

Page 21: Charles M. Blackford has written that the *Rizal* (DD-174) also had a stern winch, as did his ship, the *McDougal* (DD-54), a "thousand-tonner." He noted that when observation balloons were being towed, the up-and-down motion of the ship's stern made the air crews sick.

Page 23: HMS *Broadway* (ex-DD-194) is reported to have been named after the street in New York City. British officers were far from unanimous in admiring the flush deckers: one admiral is quoted as saying "I thought they were the worst destroyers I had ever seen, poor seaboats, with appalling armament and accommodations." Philip A. C. Chaplin has written that the *Lincoln* (ex-DD-143) was never in the Royal Canadian Navy but flew the Norwegian flag when operating, like many other Allied ships, under Canadian command at various times. Chaplin says only ten of the U.S. destroyers in addition to the seven originally transferred actually became part of the RCN. Lenton and Colledge (see bibliography addendum below) identify nine: the *Buxton* (ex-DD-265), *Caldwell* (ex-DD-133), *Chelsea* (ex-DD-134), *Georgetown* (ex-DD-168), *Leamington* (ex-DD-127), *Mansfield* (ex-DD-78), *Montgomery* (ex-DD-75), *Richmond* (ex-DD-93), and *Salisbury* (ex-DD-140).

Page 24: H. T. Lenton has identified the object on the bridge of HMS *Ramsey* (ex-DD-274) as a "perspex lantern enclosing the scanner unit for type 273 radar, a surface bearing and ranging set," not a gun director as stated in the photo caption.

Page 25: Martin Williams has written that *Mariner's Mirror* (Vol. 43, No. 2, p. 144) describes how the *Leamington* (ex-DD-127) was rescued from the scrapyard and refitted at Pembroke to play the part of the *Campbeltown* (ex-DD-131) in the film *The Gift Horse* before being scrapped at Newport in 1951. (Also see photo on page 94.)

Page 31: The *Ward*'s No. 3 gun was preserved at the Washington Navy Yard until 1958, when it was moved to the grounds of the Minnesota state capitol in St. Paul. (Also see photo on page 92).

Page 62: John Hunyadi has noted that the second-class smoking room of the liner *Leviathan* contained a painting of that ship in camouflage with the profile of a destroyer outlined on its side in an effort to deceive submarines.

Page 65: The *Williams* (DD-108) should be listed as HMCS as well as HMS *St. Clair*. F. C. Gray has written that *Yachting* magazine (April 1964, p. 156) reported the *St. Clair* was hit by the SS *Winding Gulf* in 1945 and sunk about a mile off the entrance to Westport River but was being salvaged.

Page 77: Several retired officers have said that hull numbers 200–205 were widely assumed within the Navy as intended to be destroyer leaders. If so, the plan never got far enough to leave any trace in the official records. Friedman (see bibliography addendum below) indicates that these numbers were included in the large *Clemson* (DD-186) group and were intended for Newport News. The emergency authorizations of World War I simply approved the expenditure of large amounts of money for different classes of ships without specifying numbers.

Pages 80–81: M. B. West, a crew member of the *Borie* (DD-215), has identified the torpedo-firing destroyer as the *Smith Thompson* (DD-212) and the location as off Olongapo. He says his ship recovered the torpedo.

Page 87: The entry for the *Marcus* (DD-321) should indicate that she was sunk by a torpedo, not gunfire.

Page 105: In the cross-index of Russian names, the ex-*Crowninshield* (DD-134) should be named *Dyerzki* (Saucy).

Page 107: The following sources should be added to the bibliography:

Friedman, Norman. *U.S. Destroyers*. (Annapolis: Naval Institute Press, 1982), pp. 41–63.

Goodheart, Philip. *Fifty Ships That Saved the World*. (New York: Doubleday and Co., 1965).

Lenton, H. T. and J. J. Colledge. *British and Dominion Warships of WWII*. (Garden City, New York: Doubleday and Co., 1968).

Lott, Arnold S. and Robert F. Sumrall. *USS Ward Fires First Shot WWII*. (St. Paul, Minnesota: The First Shot Naval Vets, 1983).

Pettitt, Henry G. "They Were a Class Apart," *The American Neptune*, Vol XLVI, No. 4 (Fall 1986), pp. 240–251.

1917    1955

The Naval Institute Press is the book-publishing arm of the U.S. Naval Institute, a private nonprofit professional society for members of the sea services and civilians who share an interest in naval and maritime affairs. Established in 1873 at the U.S. Naval Academy in Annapolis, Maryland, where its offices remain today, the Naval Institute has more than 100,000 members worldwide.

Members of the Naval Institute receive the influential monthly naval magazine *Proceedings* and substantial discounts on fine nautical prints, ship and aircraft photos, and subscriptions to the Institute's recently inaugurated quarterly, *Naval History*. They also have access to the transcripts of the Institute's Oral History Program and may attend any of the Institute-sponsored seminars regularly offered around the country.

The book-publishing program, begun in 1898 with basic guides to naval practices, has broadened its scope in recent years to include books of more general interest. Now the Naval Institute Press publishes more than forty new titles each year, ranging from how-to books on boating and navigation to battle histories, biographies, ship guides, and novels. Institute members receive discounts on the Press's more than 300 books.

For a free catalog describing books currently available and for further information about U.S. Naval Institute membership, please write to:

Membership Department
U.S. Naval Institute
Annapolis, Maryland 21402

or call, toll-free, 800-233-USNI.